Mom
It's with

that I'm signing my first
published book for you.
I pray it will bless you
greatly!

Love
John

CHINA INVADED
by Heaven

JOHN WATERHOUSE

authorHOUSE®

AuthorHouse™ LLC
1663 Liberty Drive
Bloomington, IN 47403
www.authorhouse.com
Phone: 1-800-839-8640

Published by AuthorHouse   09/23/2014

ISBN: 978-1-4969-4058-2 (sc)
ISBN: 978-1-4969-4059-9 (e)

Library of Congress Control Number: 2014916574

CONTENTS

ABOUT THE AUTHOR

Pastor John Waterhouse was born again through a visitation of the Lord Himself in a Mighty Pentecostal Wind from Heaven in 1987. Through a series of visions and revelations, the Lord ministered to him the Good News of Christ for salvation to all those who believe in Him. Since that time, he has only known the Pentecostal outpouring as the norm in his Christian faith. He heard the call from the Lord to preach the Gospel of Christ to all nations when he was 29 years old. While preaching in China from March 2010 until June 2011, the Lord told him that He wants a revival of the baptism of the Holy Ghost and fire. When John preaches Pentecost, it happens in every meeting, thus confirming the call of God on his life. The Lord appeared to him in a flame of fire while preaching in China, and since that time, whenever he preaches the baptism of fire, tongues of fire come upon the people's heads, the wind blows from Heaven, and divinely inspired dreams and visions occur in the lives of those present, thus fulfilling the Heavenly Fathers Promise, to pour out His Spirit upon all flesh. Over one thousand Chinese people testified to feeling flames of fire upon their heads when John preached the baptism of the fire of the Holy Ghost. John believes he heard the call from the Lord be a catalyst for a revolution in the church as we know it, through the outpouring of the Holy Ghost with Rivers of Living water, the breath of life, which is the wind of God and the burning, delivering, and cleansing fire of the Holy Ghost. As you read, expect to be catapulted into a reviving and inspiring life through experiencing the Gospel of Christ as the Lord had purposed you to from the beginning.

CHINA INVADED BY HEAVEN

China, a country where it's against the law for foreigners to preach the Gospel message of the Kingdom of God on earth as it is in Heaven. I had heard of stories of the Kingdom of God coming with power to this country and the persecution that comes along with it. I heard of Chinese evangelists being tortured and killed for the faith. I saw video's that were captured of the Chinese children and adults praying in caves all night long with tears of desperation for redemption. It reminded me of Israel when suffering in Egypt, and the Lord heard their cries. The stories intrigued me, moved me and touched the very depths of my heart and soul. I couldn't help but to cry as I watched the young children sobbing in prayer with hands uplifted towards Heaven. Why was the Lord touching me so deeply for China all of a sudden?

I'm no hero, but my heart cried out to go to those who were still suppressed from the knowledge of the Kingdom of God and share with them the Way, the Truth and the Life. I was being inspired by the Lord, for He was hearing their cry.

I moved there in 2009 and lived there for 16 months before coming home to Canada. I wrote my first book and had it printed secretly while living there. It was titled: "Let My People Go!" I was in the midst of a mighty outpouring of the Holy Spirit, seeing blind eyes and deaf ears opened in underground church meetings when I was the guest speaker. While preaching, I was writing in my spare time. I finished the book in five weeks. I was writing of the testimonies and the teaching that the Lord had me sharing with the Chinese people.

December 8, 2008, just over one year before going to China, the Lord spoke to me in my mind saying to read the seventh chapter of the book of Acts. I was surprised by this instruction and began reading it out loud. When I began reading the 34th verse, I began weeping uncontrollably. "I have seen, I have seen the affliction of my people which is in Egypt, and I have heard their groaning, and am come down to deliver them. And now come, I will send thee into Egypt." (Acts 7:34) It took me about 10 minutes to read this verse because every time I tried to read more, my weeping became uncontrollable and I could no longer speak. They weren't my tears. They were His. I had no personal attachments to the people of China at that time, but about a year later, I discovered that He had placed inside me a compassionate heart and desire to respond to that cry from within that Marxism oppressed country.

The heart of the Lord is responding to the heart cry of the Chinese believers in China. There's all kinds of challenges to doing ministry there, but when we are led by the Spirit of the Lord, all those obstacles can be bypassed. There's no mountain to high, no river too wide and no valley too deep for the Lord to invade with the Love of God. If God be for them, who can be against them? That I discovered during my time there. He made a way where there seemed to be no way, again and again. Many people were saved. Lives were changed and entire families were being transformed by the glory of the Lord while I was there. People were coming from all across China to bring their needy family members who needed a miracle. I had trained a team of about 80 members and would take up to 16 at a time to other cities and villages to preach the Gospel of the Kingdom of Heaven on earth as it is in Heaven. The Lord always showed up with His Pentecostal wind and fire and water. His Spirit was being poured out upon all flesh. The people were hearing about the Holy Ghost, being baptized, being saved, delivered and blessed in many ways. When invited for the Baptism of the Holy Ghost and fire, every person in the churches would step forward and tongues of Pentecostal fire came upon every head. I soon realized that Pentecost is an everlasting ordinance ordained by the Lord Himself, to reach all flesh with the attention grabbing demonstration of the Spirit and Power. His eternal intention, was that men, women and children abroad would put their faith in God and not in men.

Heaven invaded China with the Love of God from province to province, city to city and village to village. I am only one of the many missionaries who have ventured behind the Bamboo Curtain in an attempt to take the Gospel of Christ message to the people who are crying out for redemption so that they can freely worship the God they love without the threat of being shackled for their faith as the Jews were in Egypt. Nonetheless, I heard of and met mostly missionaries that knew nothing of the Demonstration and Power of the Holy Ghost. They were preachers of deep ties to Baptist and SDA church affiliations. They preached the Gospel message legalistically which gave them success because the Chinese people are accustomed to this kind of slave like control by their Marxist driven government. Their preaching was dry and lacked the influence and liberty of the Holy Ghost, leaving the Chinese believers struggling and feeling guilty and condemned for their lack of their self-controlled Christian life.

Regardless of the influx of the religiously minded, legalistic Christian missionaries to this country, there are still pockets of Holy Ghost filled and motivated Believers. Hundreds of Chinese Christian Believers in China are taking this message across the land today because Heaven invaded this country revealing to them the Messiah.

The Messiah is there now, just as He sent Moses to the Egyptian Pharoh to declare the Lord's decree, saying, "Let my people go so that they may worship me in the wilderness." Today, He sent His only begotten Son, saying, "Let my people go so they may worship me freely." May he raise up more Believers in Christ to go and declare His Gospel Message with a demonstration of the Spirit and of Power, that they all may put their faith in God and no longer in the men that have enslaved them for thousands of years.

As you read the following pages, you will hear about the victories and the messages that the Lord had me preach to these people. You will read about many very powerful and heart touching testimonies. I pray that your heart will be touched, your faith will rise and that the Lord will increase your confidence in His Promises for your own personal life in your country or abroad. If you have been seeking the Lord to lead you abroad to do missionary work, I hope my story will be a catalyst to launch you forward into that dream.

Luke 10:2 "Therefore said he unto them, The harvest truly *is* great, but the labourers *are* few: pray ye therefore the Lord of the harvest, that he would send forth labourers into his harvest."

My Personal Testimony

Chapter 2

My time in China had been spectacular with a mighty outpouring of the Holy Ghost like I hadn't seen since I myself met the Lord a mountain side in 1987. A woman had come to one of my weekly miracle meetings in China from a city that was three hours away by car. She had heard of the miracles that Jesus was performing each week and had a great need of healing. She had five different life threatening conditions. Her head and shoulders were bowed forwards and because of that she couldn't bend her head upwards to look at me in the eye. She was on many medications and was in pain all the time. When I prayed for her to be healed, I had heard the Lord speak to me in my mind, saying, "I'm healing her." I asked the woman how she was feeling, but she felt no different. I told her that Jesus was healing her and it didn't matter if she felt it immediately or not, but just to trust in Him now because He had told me He was healing her. It seemed that she and the six others with her came to test out the miracle stories they had heard. If she was healed, then they would know that the Lord was doing great things just as others had told them.

Her and the other six leaders that had come with her from her church that day had exchanged phone numbers with my translator, then left to drive home. Shortly after they left, they called my translator and were shouting praises on the phone telling her that the woman had been totally healed just as Jesus had told me! They then asked me to come with my ministry team to preach and lay hands on the sick and diseased in their church. I agreed and we made arrangements to go that following weekend. It had become very obvious that the Lord had been planning it all along. There were many events that led up to that one invitation and each one is extremely moving and faith building. When I share the stories in person, I often can't hold back the tears. It feels like I'm reliving the experience each time I talk about it. Only God knew that the very feelings I experienced when I had previously watched the videos of the crying Chinese people would become my own story.

Why Do I Have Great Faith For Miracles?

As a child, I was very adventurous. I loved a thrill and wasn't afraid to take risks. I loved the feeling of an adrenalin rush of which I had many in China. There was always a sense of danger and yet I had the peace that passes all understanding. What if I got caught preaching? This was on my mind often but I knew that it was my destiny to be there at that time and that gave me comfort. I didn't feel in any way that I would ever be arrested because the Lord had a work to do there and I always reminded myself that nothing bad could happen to me unless my Heavenly Father allowed it.

When my team and I went and preached at that woman's church, it turned out to be the most spectacular outpouring of Pentecost I had experienced since the time I arrived there. The outflow of Gods glory had been building up for 15 1/2 months prior to that time. We had seen many incredible things happen, including blind eyes and deaf ears opening, but nothing compared to this one event. That brings me now to my personal testimony and why I believe in miracles and why I believe in God.

In 1986 something tragic happened that changed the course of my life. I had suffered a serious head injury when assaulted on a street corner in the city where I lived. A year later, in 1987, I found myself standing on the edge of a cliff ready to end my life. While I was standing on the cliff edge, I was out of breath, very angry, disappointed and ready to die. **Suddenly, a mighty rushing wind came downwards from heaven onto earth.** (See Acts 2:1-4) The wind was loud and powerful and out of it came a voice introducing himself to me, saying, "My name, is Jesus Christ of Nazareth. If you will believe in Me, I will take away your burdens, I will remove your sorrows and grief's. I will heal you and I will give you eternal life." This word from Him stands as true today as the day I He spoke it to me. Since that day in 1987 He has taken care of me again and again regardless of my personal stumblings along the way. Surely I can now say with the apostle Paul, 2Corinthians 12:9 "And he said unto me, My grace is sufficient for thee: for my strength is made perfect in weakness. Most gladly therefore will I rather glory in my infirmities, that the power of Christ may rest upon me."

My skull had been fractured seven inches along its backside due to it's impact with the pavement when I was assaulted. I was rushed to the hospital in an ambulance and went into cardiac arrest on the way there. When I was taken into the hospital, my mother came and was told that the doctors didn't think they could save me due to the extreme trauma to my brain.

I remember her telling me that she went to the prayer room in the hospital that night and cried on her knees to Jesus, asking Him to save me. The surgery was a success, but I was left with major brain damage and loss of memory. I could no longer attend high school nor was it recommended for me to work a job. For one year I was searching for some way to make my life more meaningful. I tried working a job, but couldn't focus enough, nor remember my duties properly. I was living in a new city with my mother and grandmother and I didn't have any friends there. My party lifestyle was over never to return. I was empty and lonely. It seemed there was nothing left to make my life worth living anymore.

I began reading books about Middle Eastern Mysticism, ghosts, astral travel and anything like it in hopes of entertaining myself enough to make my life more bearable. I tried astral travelling, but never made it any further than my own imagination. I was left feeling empty with no hope and without God in my life. I spent lots of time with my grandmother playing cards and watching soap operas. That did help somewhat, but it wasn't enough. My grandmother was a wonderful woman and an incredible support to me at that time and today I miss her greatly.

One day I had become so desperate for something in my life and though I didn't believe in God at that time, I laid on my living room floor and tried so hard to astral travel in hope that I would leave my sorry life and never come back to it.

Finally after having no success, I gave up and changed my thinking. I was disappointed and angry and called out to the "unknown God", if there was such a thing. I called out to Him, asking Him if He was real and if He was, I wished He would come and save me and give me something worth living for. In my mind I felt like I was talking into the air, but in my heart, I was hoping that if there was in fact a God, He would hear my SOS and come rescue me. I told Him that if He was real, He would come to my rescue within three days and if He wasn't real, He wouldn't come at all. If He didn't come, I would have to end my life so that I didn't have to suffer anymore.

Three days passed and when I had waken up around 7am on the fourth day, I was feeling very angry that there was no God to come to my rescue. My anger quickly turned into rage. I quickly dressed, put my shoes on, left my house and headed to the bottom of the mountain side that was next to our house. When I got there I ran up through the bushes and tree branches. While running, I was breaking the branches that were obstacles to me. It seemed that I had superhuman strength. I finally ran out of breath from the running and stopped at a cliffs edge. I was surrounded by forest trees and as I looked forward, I could see a vast valley below.

I stepped forward to go over the cliff when suddenly a mighty rushing wind came down upon me. It seemed as though my body was hollow and the wind was going right through it and out the bottoms of my feet. I had never experienced a feeling like it before. All the feelings of rage lifted and I was standing still and in awe by this experience. Then I heard a male voice speaking to me, saying, "My name .... is Jesus Christ of Nazareth, and if you will believe in Me, I will take away all your sorrow and grief. I will heal you and give you eternal life. Listen to me carefully, for I am here to answer your call to me. I know your life. I know what you have been through. I know that you feel so empty and are full of despair. Nearly 2,000 years ago, I came down from Heaven as a spirit and impregnated a woman named Mary. She gave birth to me and I was raised by her. When I was 30 years old, I began to walk amongst people with a demonstration of My Spirit and Power. I am alive and am still giving demonstrations of who I am so that all people will believe in Me. Today I am giving you a demonstration of My Spirit and Power so that you will believe in Me and receive me as Your Lord and Savior. Believe in Me now with all your heart and soul and I will give you eternal life." (That's the short version of all He said the first time I met Him.)

At that moment I was so full of joy. The air around me had changed. I was walking in a new atmosphere on earth. The air was thick, soft, comforting, and alive, lifting and moving me in a different direction.. I knew I should follow Him at that moment. Actually, I felt like I wasn't in my body and yet I was. It seemed as though I was floating, but I knew my feet were still on the ground.

As I was standing there at the mountains cliff edge, I saw that there was a trail created by the animals that traveled along the mountain side. I began walking along it upwards, until I arrived at what seemed to be the highest point of the mountain. I stood and looked over the valley again and when I did, to my amazement, I saw a man-made bench so I decided to take a seat there momentarily. At that moment, the heavenly wind began rushing through me again so fast that I thought I would fall off the bench. I spread my feet apart and held onto the bench with my hands to secure my position on the bench. (See Acts 2:1-4)

What was now happening was different from earlier. Now there was information about the Kingdom of God on earth being downloaded into me as if I was a human computer that was receiving a download from another computer. He was, "enlightening the eyes of my understanding." (See Ephesians 1:8) I could understand the information but wondered how I would possibly remember it all. I said to the Lord, "Lord, I am understanding all this information you are downloading into me, but I am wondering how I am going to remember it all. It's so much information of things I was not previously familiar with at all." He replied, saying, "It's ok. You will understand it when it's the right time." All this time, the heavenly wind that was blowing through me was very loud, just as a natural wind would sound when blowing over our ears or whistling through the trees. I remember bits and pieces of the information that was being downloaded. It was amazing! He was downloading information about humanity and how it was originally created in His image, thus enabling His Spirit to dwell in us. I saw how mankind is still living in a much lower state that the image they were created in. We are blind from the truth of who we are and can only come back to the place He created us to walk in through Him. I saw that humanity is seeking to rise up to higher levels yet continually come short of His glory, leaving them spiritually helpless and empty. We were created to live in His glory and His glory live in us. We were created to live by His abilities in and through us.

Since that time on mountainside in 1987, He has revealed to me many of the things that was being downloaded into me that day on the mountainside. He has great plans for His church that we have not imagined possible but I have seen them happen in the future. I have seen many of them happen in dreams and visions when He has visited me since that time. I can hardly wait until that time comes. It will be more than a Great Revival. It will be a Great Harvest of souls for the Kingdom of God. Entire villages, cities and nations will be saved in one day, and then the end will come.

One time when the Lord visited me in my sleep, He told me that I would teach some of these things to some of His people at His chosen time. The time has not yet come, but it will. I'm sure there are others like myself that have heard similar things for the future, but I have not met them yet. The Kingdom of God is more exciting than the greatest sci-fi movie. It's greater than the deepest scientific theory. Science has made many discoveries in the realm of matter, but none in the invisible supernatural realm. Evolution is a matter of fact, but it's not a natural transformation. It's a spiritual transformation that takes place in the spirit. Darwinism is not based upon fact. It's still a theory. Spiritual evolution is seen in the changed life of those who are made a new creature in Christ. We have put on "the new man, which is renewed in knowledge after the image of him that created" us. (See Colossians 3:10) We have evolved from being led by the old nature, to being renewed in knowledge after His image. We now have the ability to follow after His

Spirit. We were in spiritual darkness, but now have seen a great Light and walk in it. The entrance of the Word of God into our hearts has enlightened our understanding to the Truth. Thus we were set free. (See John 8:31-32) It has made us spiritually clean and it continuously cleanses our flesh as we read His Words as spoken through Jesus. (See John 15:3 & Ephesians 5:26) It has rebuilt our spirit with spiritual stones. We are a New Creature in Christ. He has enabled us to walk and talk with Him. Thus His name is called: Immanuel, God with us. (See Matthew 1:21-22 & Isaiah 7:14)

What happened to me on the mountainside was not of this world. It was of the spiritual Kingdom of God; a realm that surpersedes the natural. It was the atmosphere of Heaven around me on earth. It was Jesus, the Son of God visiting me by His Spirit and revealing Himself to me.

Why did He reveal Himself to me this way?

This has been many peoples question to me, including my own. What I CAN tell you is that He revealed Himself to me for His own purpose and not my own. It wasn't my plan. It was His, therefore, I don't need to defend myself. When I was a young Believer, He visited me and spoke clearly to me about His purposes in my life. It scared me and I asked Him to choose another More Mature Believer. I said, "Lord, I cannot do these things that you are telling me about. I'm just a child. I know so little. There are so many Mature Believers. Please call them. I will stand for You always and help them, but I cannot do what you're telling me." He then would repeat to me what He called me to do. Today I still feel so unworthy to follow His call for my life, but regardless of How I Feel, He knows the way to fulfill His call in my life. My part is to follow Him.

What Happened Next Was His Full Salvation

I believed in Him when He came to me in the mighty rushing wind and told me His name and what He would do for me if I believed. It was at that moment that I was Born Again and just like most new believers, they don't really understand what just took place. All they know is that their sin and need for salvation was just revealed to them. When

I was sitting on the bench receiving downloads from His Holy Spirit, I was not learning about what happened to me. I was learning about the Kingdom of God, and things that will come to pass in His time. Included in this revealing to me was the role that Believers in Christ will play and how it will affect the world at large. What happened next is what I really wanted to know and what I really wanted to remember. He showed me the cross of Calvary.

It began like this: While I was sitting on the bench, the rushing mighty wind slowed down tremendously and I felt to stand up and look around. To my surprise, I saw that behind me was a man-made pathway filled with gravel. I then noticed there was short trimmed grass on either side of the path and I began to walk down it. I walked slowly, still feeling the wind blowing through me. After walking down the pathway about 50 feet, I noticed over a small hill to my right, that there was a church chapel. My eyes got big and I had the thought in my head, "That's where I have to go!" I continued to follow the path until it ended at the church parking lot. I saw the church building entrance and there was two monks standing outside it. As I was approaching it, the monks asked me if I needed anything. I asked them if I could go into the church. They said yes.

I entered the beautiful church and walked down the middle isle between the church pews. As I was getting close to the front row, I saw a brass pole standing with a cross on the top of it. I got on my knees before it and closed my eyes and said, "Jesus". As soon as I said His name, I began weeping profusely. It felt as though a thousand pounds was falling off my shoulders. I felt as though I was being healed from all my inner grief and sorrows.

Then there appeared a vision before me. It was my life. I watched my life appear before in like a very very wide screen movie screen. I watched it pass by in seemingly seconds and yet I understood every part of it. I saw this happen three times in a row. The first time that I saw it, I saw the Lord with me all my life. I was seeing His happiness as He watched me. The second time I saw it, I saw all the bad and hard times I went through in my life and how He was always reaching out to help me. This really touched my heart. The third time I saw it, I saw all the bad things I had done. I saw my sin and I saw how sorrowful He was as He watched me do things that were wrong. This made me feel ashamed, and I put my head down as if to hide from Him, but I knew I could not hide from Him.

I was scared that He would reject me now, but He did not. He then spoke to me, saying, "I sent my Son to die on a cross and shed His blood for the world so that I could forgive and remove it's sins." His voice was gentle and loving. It was as though He was reaching out to me while my head was down in shame. I was thinking to myself, "How can He forgive me and remove my sins because of His Son's blood? It makes no sense? I will ask Him." I then pointed to a part of my life in the vision where I had done something bad and said, "What about that. How could you possibly forgive me for that?" He then said, "My Son's blood is enough for me to forgive that sin." He put my head down again, and wondered about what else I had done that was worse, and asked Him again, saying, "What about that one? That was worse than the other. How could you forgive me for that?" Again He replied to me, saying, "My Son's blood is enough."

I continued to wonder to myself about this blood. Was it really enough? Was it enough for all that I had ever done? So I wondered to myself about what was the thing that I did in my life that I thought was the worst thing ever. I found it in the vision, and then I asked him again, saying, "What about that! What I did there was the worst thing I ever did! There's no way You could possibly forgive me of that." I was bold in asking and I was scared that He may say that this one thing was so bad that there's no redemption for me from that one thing. To my amazement, His reply was, "My Son's blood is not only enough for me to forgive those other sins. It's more than enough to forgive all of your sins."

Wow!! I was astonished, but I was still not fully convinced. I had one more question that I needed answered in order for me to be fully convinced of this redemption. I then said to Him, "I understand now that I need redemption and I understand that Your Son's blood is more than enough for me to be forgiven, but what I don't understand is, why? Why would you want to forgive me for all that I have done? I'm a bad person? You have seen my life. You know I'm bad. Why would you want to save me? Why would You send Your Son to die for me? I have done nothing to deserve it and I would never die for anyone."

His reply to me melted my heart and made me fall in love with Him. I knew I needed redemption now, but I didn't understand why He would redeem me. His answer to my last question was: "Because I love you and I want to be your Father."

Joy flooded my soul! My face began to shine and I felt every feeling of guilt for my sin fall away. Then suddenly I felt an invisible shower come over me and wash me from all the burdens I had been carrying throughout my life. It was so refreshing and felt as real as a physical natural water shower. ("Now ye are clean through the word which I have spoken to you." John 15:3) I then got up from my knees and walked out into the church parking lot and gazed upon the rolling hills and ponds that were part of the Churches yard. There were cows grazing the beautiful fields and groups of colorful flowers all around. I took a walk around there thinking about all that just happened to me and then I walked home.

When I got home, I was in for another surprise that touched me deeply. I walked in through the side kitchen door and saw my mother and grandmother there. My mother was cooking some bacon and eggs and she was smiling as bright as the sun. I asked her why she was looking so happy. She said, "We found something for you that we thought may make you feel a little better. We cut a personal ad out of the local newspaper and stuck it to the door of the fridge with a magnet."

I picked up the personal ad and read it. I was amazed to read the words that said this: "I found Jesus in my life and I pray to Him three times a day and He answers my prayers. I put this in here so that you would know that He will answer your prayers too." Once again, joy flooded my heart and soul and I went to my room, sat on the edge of my bed and began to pray to Jesus. That was the beginning of my new adventurous life.

I began sitting on my bed three times a day or more and praying to Jesus. I would take my guitar and strum a few simple chords and sing whatever came to my mind to say to Him. Mostly I was singing "Thank

You for saving my life. Thank You for giving me hope. Thank You for coming to me when I needed You most. Thank You for healing me. Thank You for Your Love for me. I love You too."

I knew that I was healed from my brain injury because He told me that if I believed in Him, He would heal me. ("Jesus said unto him, If thou canst believe, all things are possible to him that believeth." Mark 9:23) Not only did He heal me from my brain injury, but He also healed me from the multitude of allergies that I had since birth. I had been in the hospital more than once getting tested to find out what allergies I had. I was even allergic to dust. My eyes were often swollen when I was very young and more so in the Spring when all the pollen was floating around. That all changed after I believed in Jesus just as He promised me that it would.

I went back to work within nine days of meeting Him. I prayed for a job and told my mom that Jesus would get me a job in 9 days because that was the number of days He told me I would have it. It came to pass exactly that way. I was working full time in a door manufacturing plant making $15 per hour. That was good money in 1987.

Later in years, I had an MRI done and the neurologist who met with me couldn't find any evidence on the x-rays that showed I have any damage on my brain except a little scar tissue in one spot. My entire brain had been bruised severely and all he could see was a little scar tissue in one spot. It was a miracle! I wasn't losing my memory all the time as before. I could think more clearly and most of all, I had hope and a strong desire to live and have a good life.

What Next?

After I met Jesus on the mountainside, I had a strong desire to follow Him in every realm of my life, but it took me several months to understand what it meant to live a "Saintly Life". I was praying every day and seeking His purpose for my life. One day I drove into the mountains and parked my car beside a lake along the side of the road. I turned off my car and spoke to the Lord, saying, "I don't know what to do with my life. I have no aim in my life presently but I feel like there's something you want me to do. I will stay here beside this lake until you clearly tell me what it is."

I sat for a few hours, entering in and out of sleep. I kept telling Him to please communicate with me what He was wanting me to do. Finally I heard His voice inside my mind saying to me: "Go to Victoria, for I have a purpose for you there. Once you are there I will guide you." I started shouting, "Thank You!!! Thank You Jesus!!! Thank You so much for showing me what I need to do! I will go to Victoria."

I was only 18 years old at the time and had only known the Lord for about three months. I called some friends in Victoria and they welcomed me to come and stay with them until I could find a permanent home of my own. After arriving, I started to read the Bible every day and sit on the edge of my bed and talk to the Jesus. I didn't really understand what I was reading, so I began to take notes. I figured that would help me to understand what I was reading better.

One day, while I was reading at the dining room table at about 1pm, I heard the Lord speaking in my mind again. He told me to go downtown to a specific corner. Yates and Quadra St. to be exact. He told me to go there at 3:30pm and that there would be a man there who would be my mentor. I was so excited again and began shouting "Thank You Jesus!"

I arrived down at Yates and Quadra St. and just waited to see the man that I was to meet. I didn't know how I would know who he was, but I felt confident that somehow I would know. As I stood waiting, about 10 minutes went by, when suddenly, I saw a man about 100 meters down the sidewalk carrying a large wooden cross made from 4X4 wood. It looked to be about 10 feet long and the man was carrying it on his shoulder at the point where the two pieces of wood crossed over. I remember that he was walking very slowly. At that moment, I heard the thought, "That's the man! That's my mentor!"

I was so excited, that I had to control myself from running to see him. I walked calmly towards him and my face was smiling from ear to ear. As I approached the man, I said hi to him and asked him if I could talk with him. He kindly agreed to speak with me, stopped walking and placed his large wooden cross on the ground between us.

I told him I had a story to tell him, and leaning upon the cross, he grinned and asked me to share my story. As I was sharing with him, I felt such deep joy in my heart and I felt a strong connection with this preacher through our common experiences with Jesus.

I then told him that the Lord had spoken to me in my mind earlier that day, telling me to come to this very corner at this very time, to find the man who would be my mentor. The man was very pleased by my story and agreed that it was Jesus who was leading me. He then invited me to join him and his family for a pancake breakfast the following day at their home.

It turned out that the man was a pastor and was very well known in Victoria for carrying his cross. He went out several times each week and the response was incredible. I began walking with him several nights each week when he went out with a team of others who would be there praying for him and for those who would come and ask him why he was carrying the cross. It was good training ground in preparation of the ministry that the Lord was calling me to. I walked with him for about 1 year before he decided to retire from that ministry.

I was very close to that family and the church where they were the acting pastors. I was a youth leader, worship leader, and hosted a Bible study at my house for youth who accepted the Lord through his street ministry. My life had taken a sharp turn in a new direction. I now had direction and substantial goals in my life. In a short period of time I had become very dedicated to spending time in prayer and study the Bible.

When this man would carry the wooden cross along the downtown sidewalks, the public responses varied. While one would honk their horn and call out with a "Praise the Lord!" another vehicle driver would call out curses, such as, "Go to hell!" When he was walking by a restaurant, it seemed that every eye in the restaurant would be watching him as he slowly passed by. There were other times when a drunk person would threaten to assault him if he didn't get off the sidewalk with his cross, and others would pour their beer on it as he slowly passed by. Little did they know that any aggression against the cross would only cause him to stop and take it off his shoulder and rest it on the sidewalk. There could be 100 people all around him yelling and shouting at him, but he saw that as an opportunity to share the gospel in an effective way. I was always amazed by the hand of the Lord in our midst because there was never any physical harm done to him.

It was wonderful to experience seeing how the Holy Spirit guided him. When this pastor shared with the people, many would listen and would gain interest in his stories, as though he was some mystical wise man. They seemed to be embracing the experience as something enlightening or maybe they just wanted to have a new story to tell their friends. I could feel that there were angels all around us in the midst of the Presence of the Lord and that they were there to keep things in order.

We would sit in his big old Pontiac Station wagon with the cross on the roof rack while we prayed and waited for the Holy Ghost to show up with power before going out. I heard words like, "Lord, what is it that You're wanting to do tonight? You're the leader here. We are waiting for Your leading." Once He showed up with His power in our midst, we felt it and we knew that we were ready and He was ready. We never went out until He showed up with power.

One year, I had taken my youth group the one of the church members farm to have a fire in the yard. There we cooked hot dogs and marsh mellows together. I brought my guitar and we were singing praises and spiritual warfare songs to do battle for the safety of all those outside while they were trick or treating. It was Halloween night. One of the youth brought a friend they met at another churches youth night. He was so excited to meet me and share his testimony with us.

He said that one night about 6 months earlier, he and two other friends were walking downtown after having a few drinks. They were looking for the man who carried the cross because they wanted to ask him why he carried it. Everyone who spoke to the pastor always wanted to know why he carried it. They found the preacher carrying the cross in front of a McDonalds late at night. He said that they were asking him all kinds of questions. His two friends were mocking the man, while he personally felt a sincere sense of curiosity. Suddenly, in front of all their eyes, there were electrical currents sprouting up from the sidewalk all around the wooden cross. They all saw it and it freaked them out so much that they had become breathless and ran off. It seemed to sober them up and they just went home. After the many years ministry experiences I have had, the one sure thing I've learned of the Lord, is that whenever we present the Gospel of the Christ to people, the power of the Lord is present to bring a demonstration of the Spirit and of power. (See Romans 1:16 "I am not ashamed of the gospel of Christ: for it is the power of God ..." The power is in the message.)(See also Luke 5:16-17)

The night that the young man came to share his testimony with us, was a Halloween night. After he experienced seeing the lightning flashing from the sidewalk around the cross, he said that all he could think of, was, "On Monday I have to find that guy who always carries his Bible to school. I have to find him and ask him what happened to me!" That Monday morning, he looked for the young guy and found him. He told him his story of the lightning and then asked him what it meant. The young schoolmate invited him to meet his youth pastor and at that time he learned the meaning of salvation through Jesus Christ and accepted Him as his Lord and Savior.

I believe that we only saw a fraction of the souls that were ever saved or strongly influenced for salvation through that ministry. Only when we go to Heaven will we ever really know the effects that this ministry had.

I worked with this pastor for 3 ½ years and was being trained for ministry as a pastor, but really it prepared me best for ministry as an evangelist. I have a love for saving souls and today I still have this love. Nothing touches me more than seeing a person say a prayer for salvation.

As the years passed by, I had taken part in small ministries along the way. I had seen lots of miracles in my personal ministry and in other preacher's ministries, but nothing compared to what happened in China. The years in ministry before going to China were just primers meant to prepare me for going overseas. I saw more lives touched in my 16 months in China than I saw in the previous 22 years before going there. Nothing I had ever seen compared to what Jesus was doing in my midst in China. To Him be all the glory.

People often ask me what I will do now. My answer is easy. I will follow the Holy Ghost. In other words, for now, I will finish this book as He leads me to, and then wait for Him to lead me from there. I can have a lot more success when He is leading me than when I go out on my own. Of course, I will always be ready and am always willing to share the Gospel with anyone I meet, in whatever measure I am able to at any given time. Every seed we plant will grow, but what the people do with that seed is up to them.

I could have decided to go back and continue a work in China, but the Lord had another plan for me. Today, the Holy Ghost is influencing me with memories of the many mighty encounters I've had with the Holy Ghost over the years, and showing me that if I wait for His leading now, I will experience Greater demonstrations of the Spirit and Power. (See 1Corinthians 2:4-5 & Acts 16:6-10) Thus, many more people will be reached with the Gospel of Christ unto salvation than if I go ahead and plan my own way to preach it. (Acts 7:51) When I was 19 years old, he spoke to me through a senior pastor in my church at that time. That was in the day when ministers would say, "Thus saith the Lord ...." That's how he said it to me, "Thus saith the Lord ... the time will come when you will write a book that will affect the church in a large way abroad." That was 25 years ago and now the Lord has released me to write a book and have it published by a reputable publisher. Is this the book that will affect the church in a large way? Or will it be another book that I will write and publish in the future? I'm not sure of that. The only thing I'm sure of is that His Word is true and I believe in prophecy as given under the inspiration of the Holy Ghost.

It's When We Preach The Gospel Of Christ That The Signs Follow

Sometimes we wonder why there isn't a great outpouring of the Holy Spirit yet in our church and hope for it to come. (We forget about

Pentecost and assume that Pentecostal outpourings come at specified dates only, as opposed to coming when we simply follow His leading at any given time.) Pentecost had a schedule that was fulfilled approximately 2,000 years ago. Jesus came saying that the time has been fulfilled. Fulfilled for what? Fulfilled for the Messiah to come and fulfill the law and the prophets. Joel was the prophet of God that prophesied the coming outpouring of Pentecost. If we read the book of Joel carefully, we can see that Pentecost continues until the end of the world.

We sometimes think we have the formula that will be the catalyst to make it happen, but all the requirements for the Pentecostal Outpouring to come were fulfilled in Jesus Christ. He said, Luke 24:49 "And, behold, I send the promise of my Father upon you: but tarry ye in the city of Jerusalem, until ye be endued with power from on high." Matthew 5:17 "Think not that I am come to destroy the law, or the prophets: I am not come to destroy, but to fulfil." There's nothing we can do to convince Him to come with the Power of Pentecost. It's already here. He did all that needs to be done for it to happen. What we need to do is let go of all our preconceived ideas that God is waiting for a specific time to come again. We go and preach the Gospel of Christ according to His directions and demonstrations of it, then the signs will follow. (See Mark 16:15-20) It's that simple. This was what I discovered before I left Canada and especially experienced when in China. Preach what He told His disciples to preach. Not hell and brimstone. It's the Holy Ghost's job to convince people of sin, righteousness and judgement. We tell them the Good News of Christ. He does the rest by confirming that message with the Signs following.

The Lord is "not willing that any should perish, but that all should come to repentance." (See 2Peter 3:9) As we see in Revelation 21:23-24, that nations will be saved and shall walk in the light of the New Jerusalem. This is the Lord's desire. He desires entire nations to be saved, and they will be … but not by keeping the Gospel of Christ to ourselves. We want the outpouring of the Holy Ghost inside our four walls, but the place we will experience it is outside the four walls when we take the Gospel of Christ to those outside. The Signs of Pentecost follow those who preach the Word of God to all nations. That may begin in our own household and then to our neighbors and then our city and country.

Revelation 21:23-24 "And the city had no need of the sun, neither of the moon, to shine in it: for the glory of God did lighten it, and the Lamb *is* the light thereof. **And the nations of them which are saved shall walk in the light of it:** and the kings of the earth do bring their glory and honour into it."

Revelation 22:2-3 "In the midst of the street of it, and on either side of the river, *was there* the tree of life, which bare twelve *manner of* fruits, *and* yielded her fruit every month: and **the leaves of the tree *were* for the healing of the nations. And there shall be no more curse:** but the throne of God and of the Lamb shall be in it; and his servants shall serve him."

It's easy to be distracted by all the terrible atrocities that are happening around the world with groups like ISIS or Al Quada, but we need to keep our eyes upwards and do our part to save as many as possible. If ever there was a time that the world needed Signs and Wonders to believe in Jesus, the time is now.

I am presently preparing to do my part in ministry once again in Canada. Writing this book has been part of my preparation. It will be a tool for me to minister to the New Believers as they come into salvation by faith in Christ. Being a minister of the Gospel of Christ does not require us to quit our jobs and forsake our families as some perceive it to be. For me, it's a hobby and a very enjoyable hobby. I love sharing the Gospel of Christ with people wherever I am. Through the many years of sharing it, the Lord has shown me many tools to make it more effective and this book is going to help me achieve that by helping others globally prepare themselves to preach it where they live. By this means, I will be indirectly reaching hundreds to thousands of others with the Gospel of Christ outside of my own country without having to go there personally.

His Instructions While I Was Preparing For Ministry:

For 2 years, I focused hard on ministry preparation before He sent me to China. During that two years, I would come home directly from work and spend time seeking Him with praise and worship, waiting on His Presence, & studying His Word. One time, while I was waiting upon His Presence in preparation for leading worship in my church the next day, the Lord spoke to me in my mind, saying, "Tomorrow, during worship at church, I will speak to you, saying, "Declare that The Kingdom of Heaven is at hand!"

At first, I was shocked at His instruction because I had never heard any preacher preach this way before in church or otherwise. Nonetheless, He had given me specific instructions and then He gave me an example of how it would feel. Immediately I continued to wait on Him in my living room with hands uplifted. I then heard Him say, "Say it now!" So I said it, "The Kingdom of Heaven is at hand!" At that moment when I said it, suddenly a massive wave of His glory rolled over me! I could literally feel it physically roll over me as a massive wave, as if standing in the ocean shoreline when the large waves roll in. It was amazing! From that time till now, I know that every time I say that, a wave of His glory goes forth. I don't have the same feeling every time I say it, but He gave me faith to know that this is what happens every time I say it whether I feel it or not.

The next day, while in church, I told the worship team what the Lord told me to do and shared with them the testimony of how He showed me to do it while I was waiting on Him the night before in my living room. They were prepared to follow. During the worship time, I was waiting silently between songs, expecting that He would speak to me. I then heard Him say, "Say it now!" So in the midst of the silence, I yelled out, "The Kingdom of Heaven is at hand!" and wham! The same wave of His glory rolled over the entire church! You could hear the people saying things like, "Wow!" all over the church building. We stood in awe and people just began whispering praises to Him as the glory continued to roll over us. Then the praises became louder and louder as the wave of His glory continued to rise above us until we were immersed in the wave of His glory.

When I was preaching in China, in every meeting, I would preach, saying, "The Kingdom of Heaven is at hand." I always got the same results there that I had in Canada during my preparation time and more. This is the message that Jesus guaranteed to confirm with signs following. It's the Gospel of Christ which is the Power of God unto salvation for all who believe. (See Romans 1:16)

My team was used to me saying it every meeting and I would tell them to place their hands in front of them, and say, "The Kingdom of Heaven is at hand." It was as close as their hands are to them and through our declaration of it, The Lord always confirmed it was at hand with the Signs and Wonders following as He promised He would. This was my lesson with the demonstration for them and this is what I preached when we went to other cities and villages together to preach the Gospel of Christ on earth as He is in Heaven. How is He in Heaven? In Heaven, there's no more sickness, disease, sorrow or grief because they are living in His glory. It's the air they breathe. There's only the bliss of being free from all the natural burdens we experience on earth and the ecstatic feeling of the glory of the Lord. Jesus taught us to pray that He would be and operate on earth as He is and operates in Heaven. So be it! In Jesus name! (See 2Corinthians 1:20) ("Is there a law against the promises of God? God forbid." See Galatians 3:21)

They heard my training so many times they could preach it themselves and some of them still are today. One sister called me recently (August, 2014) and updated me that she left China in January and has been travelling from city to city across India and sharing the Gospel of Christ from village to village, tent to tent, city to city and province to province. The Lord has been her provision since she began with her ministry partner and it's now been 8 months since they started in India. The Lord never fails them. Thank You Jesus!

There's a way to practice this kind of preaching. You can say it while you are spending time in prayer alone in your room. Just say, "The Kingdom of Heaven is at hand." As you practice it you will see the Lord confirm it with the Signs Following. You can practice it in a Home Group or Bible Study. Invite 2 or three friends over and tell them you are starting a Home Group and practice preaching in that setting. You will be amazed at what you see. These are some of the ways that I practiced and still practice today.

I find that there are times when I think I'm doing the will of God in my life, but the Lord puts a stop to what I'm doing, by graciously revealing to me that I am out of step with Him. I may suffer financial loss at that moment, or otherwise, but at least I recognize it and He helps me to get back on track with Him again. Let's not get down upon ourselves when it seems we are out of line. We just need to keep coming to Him, stand up or sit down and keep moving forward.

Join the worship team, or volunteer to participate in the youth group but never get so attached that you follow the leading of men rather than the leading of the Holy Ghost. Help in the kitchen ministry, or anywhere you can and you will then find more opportunities to see the glory of the Lord flow through you.

When you pray for someone in church or elsewhere, just say, "The Kingdom of Heaven is at hand" as part of your prayer. We are releasing the glory of God when we do this. These were Jesus' instructions and demonstrations and therefore it's a sure thing. It's not a method, it's an instruction from the Lord Jesus Christ and it's not based upon a feeling. Nonetheless, the feeling WILL FOLLOW, when he confirms His Word with the Signs following.

Another word of wisdom is, that you don't share with others everything that the Lord is sharing with you. You may have one person or more that's close enough for you to share with, but I can tell you honestly from my own experience and the experience of other ministers I know very well, that when you share too much with others, you will find the people you know and think will support you may be the ones to scrutinize you. Just be careful who you share with.

The thing I love the most, is when I feel the glory of the Lord. I just think about His glory and it's there. A smile comes on my face and it brings with it the peace that passes all understanding. We may feel heavy, upset, or overwhelmed by the circumstances that we are presently facing, but when we think about His glory, it comes tangibly; and when it comes, it brings freedom, by lifting the burdens, griefs and sorrows, giving me the rest we so desperately need. He said that if we are heavy due to our heavy labour or otherwise, to come to Him, and in return,

He would come to us and lift the burden. We can come to Him all day long, no matter what we are facing. He's always there. He's always at hand. We just remind ourselves about His glory that's living inside of us, and just as a magnet is drawn to metal, even so His glory is drawn to us. James 4:8 says, "Draw nigh (Gr. near) to God, and he will draw nigh to you."

HE IS THE WORD OF GOD
Signs And Wonders
The Baptism Of Fire

Chapter 3

In the Gospel According to John, we see that Jesus is "The Word of God" that was made flesh. He came as a shining light from Heaven. People saw His glory radiating from Him and were drawn to it. "We beheld his glory." The Word of God is the highest authority in the universe, therefore it's so important that we understand why and how it touches and enlightens us as we read it by faith.

John 1:1-14
"In the beginning was the Word, and the Word was with God, and the Word was God. The same (Word) was in the beginning with God. All things were made by him (The Word); and without him (The Word) was not any thing made that was made. In him (The Word) was life; and the life (The Word) was the light of men. And the light (The Word) shineth in darkness; and the darkness comprehended (Gr. To take eagerly, attain) it not. There was a man sent from God, whose name *was* John. The same came for a witness, to bear witness of the Light (Word), that all *men* through him (The Word) might believe. He was not that Light, but *was sent* to bear witness of that Light. *That* was the true Light, which lighteth every man that cometh into the world. He (The Word) was in the world, and the world was made by him, and the world knew him not. He came unto his own, and his own received him not. But

as many as received him, to them gave he (The Word gave) power to become the sons of God, *even* to them that believe on his name: Which were born, not of blood, nor of the will of the flesh, nor of the will of man, but of God. And the Word was made flesh, and dwelt among us, (and we beheld his glory, the glory as of the only begotten of the Father,) full of grace and truth." (Brackets added by myself)

Jesus is the Divine Expression of God Himself. He is the arm of God revealed to the world. (See Isaiah 53:1 "To whom is the arm of the LORD revealed?" We are His mission field and He is still working amongst us in our midst to accomplish His eternal goal to bring mankind out of spiritual darkness and into His Divine Light. ("And the hand of the Lord was with them: and a great number believed, and turned unto the Lord." See Acts 11:21)

The Word of God is Spirit, Light, Knowledge and Wisdom and we are enlightened in our understanding upon its entrance into our spirit. He gave us spiritual ears to hear so that our understanding can be open and we receive spiritual and physical nourishment from it. By His Holy Spirit, He guides us into all Truth. His Word is Truth. (See John 16:13 & 17:17) He is the Word and He is the Way, Truth and the Life. (See John 14:6) In Him was Life and the Life was and IS the Light of men (mankind).

Hebrews 1:1-3
"God, who at sundry times and in divers manners spake in time past unto the fathers by the prophets, Hath in these last days spoken unto us by his Son, whom he hath appointed heir of all things, by whom also he made the worlds; Who being the brightness of his glory, and the express image of his person, and upholding all things by the word of his power, when he had by himself purged our sins, sat down on the right hand of the Majesty on high."

When we read out loud the Words spoken by Jesus, Living Water is released from our spirit and poured out upon our flesh, cleansing us, sanctifying us, and quenching our thirst. When we speak the Words of Christ to others, the Living Water is released upon their flesh, washing them, cleansing them, and quenching their thirst. (See John 7:37-39)

His Words are spirit and life. They are life giving words. They are eternal life.

John 6:63, 68

"It is the spirit that quickeneth (Gr: "make alive, give life; by spiritual power to arouse and invigorate"); the flesh profiteth nothing: the words that I speak unto you, they are spirit, and they are life." Verse 68 "Then Simon Peter answered him, Lord, to whom shall we go? Thou hast the words of eternal life."

John 15:3-4A

"Now ye are clean through the word which I have spoken unto you. Abide (Gr. Remain) in me, (The Word, The Light of men) and I in you."

Ephesians 5:25-27

"Husbands, love your wives, even as Christ also loved the Church, and gave himself for it; That he (The Word) might sanctify and cleanse it with the washing of water by the word, that he might present it to himself a glorious church, not having spot, or wrinkle, or any such thing; but that it should be holy and without blemish."

According to what the apostle Paul said to the Ephesians, The Word of God is what washes His Church, His Bride in preparation for the Great Wedding feast with Him, our Bride Groom. When we struggle to live a good life that reflects Christ in us, we need to get back to The Word of God which washes and cleanses us from the immorality that tries to cling to us in the world. It also reminds us of our legality in Christ against the oppression of the devil that tries to ensnare us in his traps.

This outpouring of His Spirit through His Words is a fulfilment of prophecy concerning Him as spoken by the prophet Joel:

Acts 2:15-20

"For these are not drunken, as ye suppose, seeing it is but the third hour of the day. But this is that which was spoken (The Prophetic Word) by the prophet Joel; And it shall come to pass in the last days, saith God, I will pour out of my Spirit upon all flesh: and your sons and your daughters shall prophesy, and your young men shall see visions, and your old men shall dream dreams: And on my servants and on my handmaidens I will pour out in those days of my Spirit; and they shall prophesy: and I will shew wonders in heaven above, and signs in the earth beneath; blood (The blood of the Lamb of God), and fire (The pillar of Fire returning into our midst), and vapour of smoke (The visible manifestation of the glory of God): The sun shall be turned into darkness, and the moon into blood, before that great and notable day of the Lord come."

When we have this understanding of the supernatural life that we are releasing upon ourselves and others when reading His Words, we become hungrier to read it every day. If we don't understand the spiritual implications of reading it out loud, then we become tired and distracted when reading it and it feels more like a chore than a spiritual blessing (See Ephesians 1:3). His Words are spirit and they release Living Water to cleanse us, sanctify us and quench our thirst. (See John 4:14 & 7:37-39) They release the spiritual blessings upon us and rejuvenate us with joy and peace and fill us with His glory. (See Ephesians 1:3 & Philippians 4:6-7 & 1Peter 1:8)

He cleanses His church, meaning its members, with His Word. Paul uses this example to show us how we should love our wives. We love them by sharing the Word with them. It releases Living Water upon them, sanctifying and cleansing them. Happy wife, happy life! So all you men out there, if you want to improve your marriage, begin by sharing the Word of God with them. The same thing applies to our children. If we want to help our children to do well in life, we need to share the Word of God with them in a fun and loving way. Teach them what happens when they hear it. They generally have better imaginations than us. You can share the Word at the dinner table each night after eating. Each can share a portion or give the responsibility to one person each night to read a portion, take one or two minutes for everyone to close their eyes and ask the Lord to reveal it to them. Then ask everyone if the Lord spoke anything to them about what the verse or verses means for them. Teach them to guard the word in their hearts as a treasure from God. This is just one suggestion for those who may be wondering how they could possible minister the Word to their family. It could also be done at night time as your children are going to bed.

Making a consistent reading time will help your children to learn to trust in God and experience Him answering their prayers.

I like sending scriptures as text messages to friends as I am inspired. I am cooperating with the Holy Spirit when doing this. It's so much fun! He puts a scripture in my mind to send to a specific person. It often turns out to be exactly what they needed to hear at that moment.

The Word is Like Medicine:

When we have a pain, we may take a pain killer tablet to ease it. The Word of God is like this. We call it the Gospel, meaning The Good News. For fun we can call it "The Gos-pill". As soon as we hear the Words of Jesus, they enter into our flesh house and begin to remove the source of the pain. The Words of Jesus "sanctify and cleanse" our flesh. They're "spirit and life." By speaking the Words of Jesus out loud, we are releasing His spiritual power that arouses and invigorates us. His Words were powerful when He spoke them through His flesh body on the earth. They are still powerful when we speak them by faith. The Words of Jesus are still the words of Jesus and we are His flesh on earth. Through us, His body, He continues all that He began to do while on earth in His earth suit. We are now His earth suit and through us He extends Himself. He shines the Light of His Word through us. He is the Light of the World.

Proverbs 10:11 "The mouth of a righteous *man is* a well of life: but violence covereth the mouth of the wicked."

Proverbs 18:21 "Death and life *are* in the power of the tongue: and they that love it shall eat the fruit thereof."

When we take a pain killer, we don't think about how it works in our system. We don't use our brains to direct it to the source of the pain. So is the Word of God. We don't need to give it directions. We just hear the Word, and it goes to work on our behalf. It knows what to do.

I read the Words of Jesus every day. I will begin my day by reading some of His Words in one of the Gospels and because I already have the understanding of the power of His Words, when I read them out loud, it goes to work on my behalf immediately. I print my own Word brochures on certain topics, and take that with me to work each day. I read it when I'm travelling to work and on my breaks I read through them out loud. They arouse and invigorate me by the joy of the Lord. (See

John 15:7
"If ye abide (remain) in me, and my words abide in you, ye shall ask what ye will, and it shall be done unto you."

His spiritual blessings are active in us when we abide in His Word. They bless us in every realm of our lives. We don't need to direct them to the specific area of need. They know the need and they know how to provide for that need. We simply need to activate those spiritual blessings by reading His Words out loud to ourselves daily. This is a key to the kingdom of God that's within us. (See Matthew 16:19 "And I will give unto thee the keys of the kingdom of heaven …")

The Word "abide" means: "to stay … remain … continue … dwell … be present … tarry" In Psalm 91:1, we read of the power of remaining in Him and Him remaining in us.

Psalm 91:1
"He that dwelleth in the secret place of the most High shall abide under the shadow of the Almighty."

As we spend time in His Word each day, we are abiding in the secret place of the most High, and in doing so, we are kept safe from the traps that come against us and if they do ensnare us on occasion, His Words will deliver us.

The secret place is called "secret" because it's out of sight from the destroyer. It's the place where we are hidden from the traps of the enemy of our soul. He can't touch our soul, because it's hidden in Christ in the heavenly places, but he will try to attack our flesh or things that are important to us. The thing is, that as long as we abide in Him, a "hedge of protection" is placed around us and our belongings. It's when we come out of the hedge of protection that we become a vulnerable target. (See Job 1:10)

Proverbs 30:5
"Every word of God is pure: he is a shield unto them that put their trust in him."

The apostle Paul admonishes us to be strong in the Lord and in the power of His might by putting on the whole armour of God so that we can stand against the whiles (Gr. "trickery") of the devil.

In Paul's list of the armour of God, he makes mention of the Word of God as a form of defensive and offensive armour, saying, "take the helmet of salvation, and the sword of the Spirit, which is the word of God". (See Ephesians 6:10-18)

The helmet of salvation and the sword of the Spirit are the Word of God. The helmet is the "peace of God" that guards our heart and mind in Christ Jesus. (See Philippians 4:6-7) That's part of our defensive armour. The sword of the Spirit is our defensive and offensive armour. So the Word of God is our shield and our sword. (See also Deuteronomy 33:29)

Jesus used the sword of the Spirit when casting out devils and healing the sick. ("He cast out the spirits with his word, and healed all that were sick." See Matthew 8:16-17 "He sent His word and healed them and delivered them from their destructions." See Psalm 107:20) As soon as the Word goes out of our mouth, it begins working, just like a seed once planted begins to germinate after being in a period of dormancy. It's also like a chicken egg that's been incubating under the heat of a hen. The Word is planted into our spirit and incubates. We don't need to feel it working in order for it to begin working. When the farmer plants his seeds in the ground, he doesn't come to see the soil every day to observe if they are working or not. He keeps watering the soil and cleaning out the weeds around them, knowing that they are growing. (See Matthew 4:26-33)

His Word is Creative in our mouth. "God said, Let there be light: and there was light." (See Genesis 1:3) It was when God SAID, "Let there be light" that there was light. His Word remained dormant as long as it was only in His mind. It wasn't until He spoke His Word that it began to germinate. So the Word of God remains dormant. How do we effectively speak the Words of God? Simply read the Words of Jesus out loud. Do it quietly if you like. As we do that, we are releasing the Spirit of His Word and it immediately begins to grow in us with the intent of bringing forth a harvest.

When Jesus was being tempted by Satan during His 40 day fast, He spoke the Word of God in defense. He didn't just think the Word of God. He spoke it and when He spoke it, it not only acted as a shield to Him, it was a sword that defeated Satan, and Satan left after Jesus quoted only three verses. See Ephesians 3:10, which says, "To the intent that now unto the principalities and powers in heavenly *places* might be known by the church the manifold wisdom of God.") That's the Power of the Word of God. The Word of God was already in His heart and therefore was very fruitful when He spoke it. He was and is the Word of God that was made flesh. The Word of God, as we speak it becomes flesh in us. We are not the Word of God, but the Word of God becomes flesh in us as we plant it through speaking it. As Paul says to the Romans, that faith comes from hearing and hearing the Word of God, not by having read it. (See Romans 10:17) So faith is imparted through the planting of the Word of God into our hearts. (See Romans 10:8, which says, "The word is nigh thee, *even* in thy mouth, and in thy heart." & 2Corinthians 3:3 which says, "Written not with ink, but with the Spirit of the living God; not in tables of stone, but in fleshy tables of the heart.")

The Word, once planted into our hearts is revealed to us by the Holy Spirit. It's not understood with our intellect. He is the one who opens our understanding.

When I was a new believer in Christ, I knew that I could defend myself with the Word of God, but I wondered how I would know which Word of God to use in my defense or as an offensive measure at any given time. When we abide in the Word and the Word abides in us, we will know all things at the needed time. The Holy Spirit is the one who speaks in our defense through us and as our offense. After all, it's the "sword of the Spirit" and He is here to "guide us into all truth." He even prepares us ahead of time, by "showing us things to come". He will guide us into the truth of The Word of God that we will need before we need it. (See John 16:13) This is also referred to as "prophecy". He speaks to us prophetically, showing us things to come. Through this kind of fellowship with the Holy Spirit, we are inspired to continually praise and worship Him. We experience Him leading us and blessing us and we get excited about it. We realize that we are not alone, but He is alive and living in us. It's "Christ in us, the hope of glory." (See Colossians 1:27)

The Early Church Had The Words of Jesus:

It's important that we don't assume that everything preachers tell us is accurate. I'm speaking for myself as well when I say this and I say it because as long as I personally have allowed myself to believe most everything they taught, I was limiting myself from hearing from the Holy Spirit directly in all of my studies of the Words of God. I spent several years going from famous preacher to famous preacher and buying their CD's, DVD's and books and trying to learn the Word of God. Some of what they said was good but there's was always contradictions between them and one attacked the others teaching. It confused and discouraged me and caused me to struggle in my own relationship with the Lord. It took me years to get back on track and learn to rely upon the Lord's directions for me. I'm not saying preachers should be avoided, I'm just pointing out that we should spend more time in our Bibles and listening to the Holy Ghost as He leads us into all truth, and less time going from preacher to preacher. The preachers are meant to train us for the work of the ministry. They are meant to be our helpers in ministry. (See Ephesians 4:11-15)

It's been preached by many that in the early church, they never had the New Testament writings to help them. It's been assumed that they only had the use of the Old Testament scriptures to preach from. This is false. They had the teachings of Jesus which is the basis for the New Testament that we have today. They were making copies of the Gospel message and sending them all over the world. They in fact had more writings than we have today.

Acts 10:37-38

"That word, I say, ye know, which was published throughout all Judaea, and began from Galilee, after the baptism which John preached; How God anointed Jesus of Nazareth with the Holy Ghost and with power: who went about doing good, and healing all that were oppressed of the devil; for God was with him."

Luke shared, saying, "Forasmuch as many have taken in hand to set forth in order a declaration of those things which are most surely believed among us, Even as they delivered them to us, which from the beginning were eyewitnesses, and ministers of the word." (See Luke 1:1-2) We can see from this that there were many eyewitnesses and ministers of The Word of God in their time who were sharing it and publishing it with the demonstration of the Spirit and with power. (See 1Corinthians 2:4)

Isn't it interesting that as we read the New Testament Gospels as written by Matthew, Mark, Luke and John, that they were not preaching the Old Testament as a present day service, but rather, they were preaching Jesus Christ as the fulfilment of it. They used the odd Old Testament reference foreshadow to confirm the New. I expect that it took the disciples years to accumulate the full understanding of Who Jesus really was according to the Old Testament scriptures. (For example, see Matthew 8:16-17) So how is it that some today are saying they preached from the Old Testament only and that all they had then was the Old Testament scriptures? It's amazing how easily we are misled. I don't say this to condemn anyone, including myself, for I have preached the same thing under the assumption that what they were teaching was correct. I say this to help us open our eyes to the truth in all that we hear regarding Jesus Christ. We should read it for ourselves and allow the Holy Spirit to guide us.

The holy apostles, prophets and disciples of Jesus were preaching the Words and Testimonies of Jesus' ministry abroad. (See Ephesians 3:5) This is how they were releasing the Rivers of living water to the nations. It was by the Words of Jesus that they were preaching under the inspiration of the Holy Spirit and confirmed by the hand of the Lord in their midst. (See Acts 4:8, 31; John 5:32) These were the Words that Jesus confirmed with signs following.

John 7:37-39
"In the last day, that great day of the feast, Jesus stood and cried, saying, If any man thirst, let him come unto me, and drink. He that believeth on me, as the scripture hath said, out of his belly shall flow rivers of living water. (But this spake he of the Spirit, which they that believe on him should receive: for the Holy Ghost was not yet given; because that Jesus was not yet glorified.)" NOTE: The words in brackets above are in fact what's written in the book of John. I didn't add those words. Since we were Born Again and Baptized with the Holy Ghost, we have become a well of Living Water, from which the Holy Ghost Living Water pours out. Jesus said, "Out of his belly (which is speaking of your spirit) shall flow rivers of living water." Rivers. Not a single river, but rivers, plural.

Proverbs 10:11 "The mouth of a righteous *man is* a well of life."

The Shadow Of Christ - Our Rock Of Salvation – The Living Water

"Jesus stood and cried, saying, If any man thirst, let him come unto me, and drink." (See John 7:37)

Christ is the Rock of Salvation, 1Corinthians 10:4 "And did all drink the same spiritual drink: for they drank of that spiritual Rock that followed them: and that Rock was Christ."

Exodus 17:6 "Behold, I will stand before thee there upon the rock in Horeb; and thou shalt smite the rock, and there shall come water out of it, that the people may drink. And Moses did so in the sight of the elders of Israel." It was the Lord, the Christ that stood upon the rock and confirmed His Word to Moses. Living water came out of that rock. That was a type and shadow of the things to come. It was prophetic and Jesus came to fulfill that prophecy. Now that Well of Living Water is in us and flows from our spirit as we minister the Word of God to others and to ourselves. "It's Christ in us, the hope of glory." (See Colossians

1:27) "He that believeth on me, as the scripture hath said, out of his belly shall flow rivers of living water." When does it come out? When we share the Gospel of Christ. That's when it's released from the well within us to others. As we read the Word of God it's also released upon all our flesh.

John 4:13-14 "Jesus answered and said unto her, Whosoever drinketh of this water shall thirst again: But whosoever drinketh of the water that I shall give him shall never thirst; but the water that I shall give him shall be in him a well of water springing up into everlasting life."

Psalm 95:1 "O come, let us sing unto the LORD: let us make a joyful noise to the rock of our salvation."

There's Healing In The Rivers

Revelation 22:1-2 "And he shewed me a pure river of water of life, clear as crystal, proceeding out of the throne of God and of the Lamb. In the midst of the street of it, and on either side of the river, *was there* the tree of life, which bare twelve *manner of* fruits, *and* yielded her fruit every month: and the leaves of the tree *were* for the healing of the nations." I don't understand how the river was in the midst of a street, but on either side of the river it says that there is the tree of life, which bare twelve manner of fruits: and the leaves were for the healing of the nations. We can be sure that the rivers that are coming out of our bellies as we continually come to Christ and abide in His Word are coming from this river in Heaven. In that river is the leaves that are for the healing of the nations. We can then conclude that there's healing power in the river for nations. As we preach the Gospel of Christ, to ourselves or others, there's healing being released in the river just like tea leaves saturate hot water.

Pre-requisites To His Words Being Powerful

There ARE pre-requisites to the Words of God being powerful in our mouths. The first and most obvious, is that we must be Born Again and we must be filled with the Holy Ghost. "Except a man be born again, he cannot see the kingdom of God..." (See John 3:3-5) (See Acts 4:31

"And they were all filled with the Holy Ghost, and they spoke the word of God with boldness."

It's the Words of Jesus that are not a shadow of things to come. They were and are the Light of mankind. They are the Spirit of Christ being released into this world. When spoken, they are spirit and they are like the wind … they come and go as they please when released by our mouths.

If we want to have signs following our ministry, we need to speak the Words of Jesus in our preaching. One day when I was on my way to one of the Tuesday weekly miracle services, I heard that still small voice of the Lord say to me: "If you preach what I preach, you will get the same results I get."

Well, I was already getting good results preaching what He preached but then I realized that when I was preaching I would digress into some of my own ideas as well. The Lord was aiming at maximizing the results I was getting for His glory and minimizing mine.

A Fire Went Before Him

The Lord visited the children of Israel with great power (fire-glory), delivered them from Egypt and brought them into the wilderness for forty years before bringing them into the Promised Land. Everything He did in delivering them by His manifested glory in their midst was a type and shadow of what Christ would do to deliver people today with great power (fire-glory). (See Luke 5:17, which says, "The power (fire-glory) of the Lord was present to heal them.") The fire over the tent in the wilderness was the same fire that came to be hosted by the church in this age. (See Acts 7:37-38 & Numbers 9:15) "This is he, that was in the church in the wilderness with the angel which spake to him in the mount Sina." Acts 7:38 "There was upon the tabernacle as it were the appearance of fire, until the morning." Numbers 9:15

The Gospel of Christ is the Gospel of Power - Fire - Glory. It's the kingdom of God - Heaven at hand and in us … Romans 1:16 says: "For I am not ashamed of the gospel of Christ: for it is the power (fire-glory) of God unto salvation to every one that believeth; to the Jew first, and also to the Greek." The Fire is Christ and it IS the Fire/Glory of God that was with the church in the wilderness and is with, on and in every True Believer that will accept it and walk in it today. He is so wanting to release His glory upon His church and through His church to the nation's but without the knowledge of it the church has little affect to nations. They save only a small number of people in comparison to the number of those who still need to hear the Gospel of Christ.

Today children are losing interest in church on a huge scale. Churches are closing more than they are opening. Churches can't pay the mortgages or building repairs because they can't raise enough money. The church in general doesn't have much appeal to this generation. It lacks the power that belongs to True Believers in Christ. The Power that saves us is the same power that keeps us. If we don't come in by the glory, what will keep us? Do we bring them in with good music and entertainment? The music and entertainment won't save us and won't keep us. Only the glory will save and keep us. For the past 25 years, I have met believers that were part of a great movement of young people with lots of music and dancing. The youth came and sometimes this lasted for years, but the question is, what happens to the youth outside the music and hype? Do they live for Christ now? Or did they just enjoy the synergy of being amongst others of their age and having some fun? I have seen these groups come and go. I have seen them live and after time they just sizzled out. The youth generally lost all interest in going to church aside from that because it's not church they're really interested in. It's the friendships they were experiencing.

A fire went before them and consumed their enemies before they entered Jericho, the promised land. (See Deuteronomy 9:1-3 for the full story) **Deuteronomy 9:1** "Hear, O Israel: Thou *art* to pass over Jordan this day, to go in to possess nations greater and mightier than thyself, cities great and fenced up to heaven, A people great and tall, the children of the Anakims, whom thou knowest, and *of whom* thou hast heard *say*, Who can stand before the children of Anak! Understand therefore this day, that the LORD thy God *is* he which goeth over before thee; *as* a consuming fire he shall destroy them, and he shall bring them down before thy face: so shalt thou drive them out, and destroy them quickly, as the LORD hath said unto thee." (To read more about the giants, read Deuteronomy chapter 3)

These words, along with many others concerning the Fire of God, were an inspiration to me often before and while I was in China. The Lord drew my attention to them, revealing to me that "He IS a consuming fire" that was with me and was with me to destroy the darkness and it's works in peoples lives. (See Deuteronomy 4:24; 9:23; Hebrews 12:29; Exodus 24:16-17; 3:2; Isaiah 29:6; 30:27; 30:30; 33:14; Judg. 6:21; Act 7:30) There are many more scriptures that testify to the Lord as fire. Just type in the word "fire" on your search box in your electronic Bible program and you will find many matches.

Exodus 24:16-17 "And the glory of the LORD abode upon mount Sinai, and the cloud covered it six days: and the seventh day he called unto Moses out of the midst of the cloud. And the sight of the glory of the LORD *was* like devouring fire on the top of the mount in the eyes of the children of Israel."

When I was baptizing New Believers with the Holy Ghost and fire, they felt tongues of fire on their head. Every one of them felt it. Over 1,000 baptisms of fire took place in the time I was there. Signs appeared in the sky once when preaching in a village church. People began weaping and fell to their knees and worshipped God with uplifted hands.

Numbers 9:15-16 "And on the day that the tabernacle was reared up the cloud covered the tabernacle, *namely,* the tent of the testimony: and at even there was upon the tabernacle as it were the appearance of fire, until the morning. So it was alway: the cloud covered it *by day,* and the appearance of fire by night."

The tabernacle of the O.T. was a type and a shadow of us today. We today are the tabernacle of the Lord and over us rests His cloud and fire. (See Mark 9:7, Acts 1:8; 2:1-4; Luke 24:49)

The Old Testament came short of the glory of God. They fell back into sin and followed after other gods continuously. Jesus, WHO IS the glory of God, came to BRING the glory of God into the natural. He is a spirit and He took upon Himself flesh and the people beheld the glory of God on Him. He was opening eyes to SEE the glory of the Lord. Matthew 3:16 "And Jesus, when he was baptized, went up straightway out of the water: and, lo, the heavens were opened unto him, and he saw the Spirit of God descending like a dove, and lighting upon him." (Also see Mark 9:1-7; Acts 1:9-11; 7:55-56)

We Talk Like He Talked

We preach and teach the Good News that Jesus preached and taught. We speak the words He spoke. That's the message that has Signs following. (See Mark 16:15, 20 "Go ye into all the world and preach the Gospel to every creature.") He was preaching the anointing was upon Him to set the captives free. It's called by the apostle Paul, "The gospel of Christ." (See Luke 4:18 & Romans 1:16) We preach the anointing upon Him. That was His message! He preached the power of the Kingdom of Heaven at hand. THEY preached preached the Gospel of Christ, meaning, the Gospel of the anointing - the power - the Kingdom of God. (See Acts 10:37-38 "That word, I say, ye know, which was published throughout all Judaea, and began from Galilee, after the baptism which John preached; How God anointed Jesus of Nazareth with the Holy Ghost and with power: who went about doing good, and healing all that were oppressed of the devil; for God was with him.") Jesus preached that the Spirit of the Lord was upon him and anointed him to preach Good News. This is the Gospel of Christ, amd the message that He guaranteed us He would confirm with Signs following when we His disciples preached it. The Gospel of Christ IS THE POWER OF GOD UNTO SALVATION. (See Romans 1:16 KJV) He had and still has the Holy Ghost and Power upon Him to Save. He's the same today as He was yesterday. (See Hebrews 13:8)

Jesus said that we would receive the same power upon us. (See Acts 1:8; John 14:12; 20:21). It's the Power of the Holy Ghost, which was "the Kingdom of God at hand" before Jesus' resurrection. (See Matthew 12:28)

After His resurrection until now, it's not only at hand, it's within us just as it was in Him. It's "Christ in us, the hope of glory." It's the anointing in us. (See Colossians 1:27) That's the Gospel of The Power of God IN

US, for Christ is the Power of God. (See also Luke 17:21 "For, behold, the kingdom of God is within you.")

Jesus Empowers Us

Jesus gave power to His disciples in that day. Mark 3:15 "And to have power to heal sicknesses, and to cast out devils." We are His disciples in our day and He gives us power to heal the sick and to cast out devils. (See Mark 16:15-20)

His Burning Devouring Glory

He gave them His burning devouring glory then. He gives US His burning devouring glory now. (See Exodus 24:17; John 17:22) It's His devouring fire upon us that burns up sickness and disease and destroys devils. The Devils can't stand in the tormenting fire. (See Matthew 8:29 "What have we to do with thee, Jesus, thou Son of God? art thou come hither to torment us...") The Devils could see the burning devouring fire of God upon Jesus and we're afraid of being tormented. So it is when they see us with the burning devouring fire upon us. This is why the devil tries to blind God's people from knowing the truth of The Devouring Glory of God in and upon us.

Fire Balls In My Hands

One Sunday morning at church, during the worship time, something awesome happened to me and I didn't know how to respond to it. My eyes were closed and my hands were in a receiving position with the palms of my hands facing upwards at the sides of my waist. I was about 22 years old at the time. Suddenly, I felt balls of fire about the size of a baseball in the palms of my hands. They were rolling in a still position. I didn't know what it meant and I didn't know what to do, so I whispered in my pastor's ear, who happened to be standing to my right hand side and told him what I was experiencing. I asked him what I should do. He had no idea and didn't ever mention it again. I just kept my hands in that position for the longest time and could feel the balls of fire burning so hot in my hands and was asking the Lord what He wanted me to do. I had the thought that I should throw them into the crowd in the church, but I was too nervous thinking, "What if I throw my hand like that and nothing happens? People will question my action." I never threw it and eventually they dissipated.

About five years later, I was laying on top of my bed in prayer in the middle of the day. Suddenly I felt the fire balls come back again, only this time, they weren't on the palms of my hands, they were inside my body and I could feel them moving about the inside of me as though my body was hallow. It was shortly after that that I met my friend who was freshly experiencing the baptism of fire. I had never heard anything about anyone experiencing the fire besides myself, only this guy was experiencing it in a larger degree than I had. Sometimes I thought I was a little bit slow when it came to the things of the Lord. It seemed I had so many visitations but didn't know what to do with it most of the time, but this guy, for some reason, he went with it and studied it thoroughly in the Bible after he experienced it once. I hadn't done that. If I had, maybe the results would have been different. Nonetheless, the gifts and callings of God are without repentance, and the Lord made the way for me to get more understanding of it when I met this guy and we became friends. I will talk more about that experience later in the book.

I believe that there's a tremendous outpouring of the Holy Ghost that's sitting and waiting for His people to take hold of it. I am convinced that me and some others who have already experienced it are not the elect few that are meant to have had these encounters. If that were true, then that would make us greater than Jesus, because Jesus said, "The works that I do, shall he (us) do." He didn't say the works that He did, but He said the works that I do. That includes the works He is doing today. (See John 14:12) If we say that He will only use a Select Few to do mighty Signs and Wonders, that are greater than the greater works that Jesus said all who believe in Him shall do, then the Select Few must be greater than even Jesus? Impossible! The question is, do we actually Believe that we can do the things that He does? There are so many conflicting questions in the churches about who can do what, saying that only some can heal or only some can prophesy. Those questions hinder the freedom of the Holy Ghost to do whatever He wants to do through whomever He wants to do it. It's not the person who heals or prophesies. It's the Holy Ghost within them that does the work. We have no part it in, except to preach the Gospel of Christ. He is the one who heals the sick and diseased. He's the one who confirms the Word we preach with Signs following. When people think that they are the ones who do it, then they are falling short of the glory of God. All of us are ministers of the Lord. Some may be given a higher degree of talents than another, but we are all given talents. The person with one talent will do greater things than the person who is given five talents if he actually makes use of the one talent that he was given and if he is faithful with the one that the Lord has given him, the Lord will likely give him more. (See Matthew 25:14-29)

They Ministered In Signs And Wonders:

Jesus sent His disciples to minister in Signs and Wonders. (See Mark 16:15-20) He said, "These signs will follow those who believe." After His ascension to Heaven, they prayed for signs and wonders to follow their preaching in accordance with Jesus' instructions to them. So often preachers today put so much emphasis on scriptures like "women shouldn't teach", but they forsake the most important teachings of the Gospel Christ, like, "Ye shall be baptized with fire." Or, "Raise the dead, cast out devils, heal the sick and diseased." (See Matthew 3:11 & Acts 4:29-30) "That signs and wonders may be done by the name of thy holy child Jesus." (See also John 20:30-31) "And many other signs did Jesus in the presence of his disciples, which are not written in this book."

Today many Modern-Day-Christians are preaching not to seek Signs and Wonders. Who are the one's seeking signs and wonders? Signs and Wonders are supposed to follow our preaching. The unbelievers in the world are the ones that are seeking proof or some form of evidence of Christ's existence and Lordship. I don't blame them for seeking evidence in the midst of a world full of false Christ's and false forms of salvation. This is what Jesus' assignment is to all His Believers. Signs and Wonders were and still are the evidence that the Kingdom of God IS PRESENTLY at hand and they give credibility to our preaching about the resurrected Christ. It's the Good News of Christ, that He is here in our midst when two or three of us gather together in His name and when He is here in our midst, He is here with the anointing of the Holy Ghost and Power to set the captives free.

Signs and Wonders help people believe that Jesus is the Christ, the Son of God, just as John said in his book, saying, "But these are written, that ye might believe that Jesus is the Christ, the Son of God." (See John 20:30) More than 2/3's of what was written in the four Gospels was about the signs and wonders done that brought Him fame. Today it's the same. Signs and Wonders are God's advertising banners that He uses to bring fame to His name. (See John 6:2 "And a great multitude followed him, because they saw his miracles which he did on them that were diseased.")

John 20:30-31
"And many other signs truly did Jesus in the presence of his disciples, which are not written in this book: But these are written, that ye might believe that Jesus is the Christ, the Son of God; and that believing ye might have life through his name." Believing that Jesus is the Christ, the Son of God gives us life through His name. Amen!

Is it any wonder why Satan has condemned Signs and Wonders in the church today? It's because Signs and Wonders are the very thing that are used to confirm the Good News we preach, that Jesus is anointed with the Holy Ghost and Power and is going about doing good and healing all that are oppressed of the devil. For God is with Him! Hallelujah!

The devil is a thief and comes to steal, kill and destroy and He always puts a question on the Word of God. He was that way in the beginning with Adam and Eve and he hasn't changed. Today, he still goes about as a roaring lion with the question, "Did God Say That!? I doubt it." He's not our friend. He's our enemy. We should treat him as such. (See John 10:10) He's succeeded in deceiving many Modern-Day-Christians into believing that Jesus has changed but Jesus is the same yesterday, today and forever. (See Hebrews 13:8)

The Word Is Our Shield

The Word of God is our shield. When we know the truth regarding our position in Christ, we will recognize and stand firm against the tricks of the devil and conquer him. "Everyone that useth milk is unskilful in the word of righteousness: for he is a babe. But strong meat belongeth to them that are of full age, even those who by reason of use have their senses exercised to discern both good and evil." (See Hebrews 5:14-15) It means that through the application of the Word of God in our own lives, even our natural senses learn to recognize the difference between the lies and tricks of the evil one and the righteousness of God.

What Is A Sign?

A sign is something that is meant to convey information or instructions. For example: Street signs are placed along the sides of roads to guide us through traffic safely. They give us directions. The Signs of the Lord do the same thing. They get people's attention just like a street sign that may be coloured bright yellow or orange. The signs are meant to be seen. They are also called "guide posts". The Lord also uses Signs and Wonders as "Guide Posts" for people to find Him. If we are advertising our business or a community event, we may place banners in busy traffic areas to get the people's attention. We are helping them find the way to our business or event. Once they arrive, they can see the presentation, but if they can't find their way there, they may never see or hear the presentation. There are many voices in the world today that are calling out to people's spirituality. The Believers in Jesus Christ have been given the power and authority of Jesus name to create "Guide Posts" for the world through the use of Signs and Wonders.

What Is A Sign And A Wonder?

A Biblical Sign and Wonder would be healing, miracles, casting out devils, raising the dead, the wind, fire and glory clouds of the Holy Ghost showing up tangibly, visions, dreams or a prophetic word specifically to an individual or regarding an event that will take place. There are also extraordinary signs and wonders that still happen more and more frequently, such as the multiplication of food or the fragrance of His presence.

The Fragrance Of His Presence
"The Rose Of Sharon" S.S. 2:1

When I was about 29 years old, I started a full time job in a new pizza restaurant. One night when closing with the owner, I smelled a very very strong fragrance like roses. I was mopping with bleach at the time and he was cleaning the pizza making table about 15 feet away from me. I said to the Lord, "Lord, what do you want to do?" He said to me, "Show him Song of Solomon 2:1, "I am the rose of Sharon, and the lily of the valleys." But before you do, ask him what is the first thing he smells right now."

So I did it! Just as the Lord said. I walked over to him and said, "Hey John, inhale through your nose and tell me what's the first thing you smell." He smiled at me and did it. Then a big smile came on his face and he said, "I smell roses! Where's it coming from?" I said to him, "It's Jesus. He's here now and wants you to know He's real and alive and here to save you." I then grabbed my Bible and showed him Song of Solomon 2:1, "I am the rose of Sharon,

and the lily of the valleys." He read it and was amazed. For the rest of our time cleaning we could smell the strong fragrance of roses. At one point John came looking for me, saying, "Even in the refrigerator the fragrance of roses is really strong!" We were like little kids! Jesus was making Himself known in a tangible way to him and I.

The next day at work he approached me at work and said, "Remember you asked me if I ever said the sinners prayer? I thought about it all night and I can't remember ever saying it. Can you show me how to say it?" Praise the Lord! I led him in the sinners prayer.

About two days later, to my surprise, his brother in law, who also worked in the pizza restaurant approached me and told me that he loved the story about the roses and thought about for two days. He then asked me if I could help him say the sinners prayer just like John had done. It didn't end there. John's 6 year old daughter said the sinners prayer and was preaching in public. When she was in public she would tug on people's pant leg and say to the, "Excuse me! Did you know that Jesus loves you!" People would smile thinking she was so cute, and she was so cute actually. Her mother didn't feel the same way as her though and fought against it angrily, but John and her brother and her daughter just kept loving her and not fighting back, until one day ... When the mother and daughter were alone one day at home, the little girl cried out to her mother, saying, "Mommy mommy, look up there in the sky! I see Jesus standing and smiling at me!" The mother ran to the window and said, "Where! Where is He?!" And the mother saw Jesus looking down and smiling at them. The mother then wanted to say the sinners prayer too and she became very bold in preaching the gospel. John eventually took pastoral training.

The visual appearance of His glory is the next powerful manifestation that the Lord is going to administrate to draw many to His Word so that they will be open to the Good News of Christ. This is not new. It's the way the Lord manifested Himself many times in the Old Testament and its also a way that He occsssionally manifests Himself these days. I see it with my eyes open almost every time I preach, and occasionally it's visible to everyone, but the time is at hand that it will be visible to all. A good friend of mine had the fire station called and fire trucks sent to the church where he was preaching more than once. It was reported that the church roof was on fire! Why do we think God wants to hide Himself? He wants to reveal Himself to the entire world.

Exodus 3:2
"And the angel of the Lord appeared unto him in a flame of fire out of the midst of a bush: and he looked, and, behold, the bush burned with fire, and the bush was not consumed."

Exodus 24:17
"And the sight of the glory of the Lord was like devouring fire on the top of the mount in the eyes of the children of Israel.

Should the Lord be afraid that people will see His glory? Not at all! King David didn't think so when he was in the wilderness of Judah.

Psalm 63:1-2
"A Psalm of David, when he was in the wilderness of Judah. O God, thou art my God; early will I seek thee: my soul thirsteth for thee, my flesh longeth for thee in a dry and thirsty land, where no water is; To see thy power and thy glory, so as I have seen thee in the sanctuary."

When I was about 23 years old, during my pastoral training, I was invited to join my pastor and his family to a celebration that was being held in a gymnasium. They sponsored foreign students in their home several times a year and at the end of the year there was a celebration for them with food and entertainment. The foreign students were given a table to present items that they made from their culture. The Canadian families were invited to have their children share a talent. Well, that was my chance to share the gospel! So I volunteered to play my guitar and sing a song for the crowd. There was about 150 people in the celebration and each family was given a large round table to sit at. When I was invited to begin my performance, I began by telling the story of Amazing Grace Song writer, John Newton. It took only about 2 minutes to tell it and then I began playing my guitar and singing Amazing Grace. As I was singing the glory of the Lord appeared and filled the entire gymnasium in clear view to everyone! My pastor and his wife were in awe at what was happening and their eyes grew like massive marbles. I was observing it with my eyes. You could feel the thickness of it in the air. People all over the room began crying. The glory was in the appearance of water, as if we were sitting at the bottom of a large swimming pool. The glory was rippling and moving just as you would expect the water in the ocean to move with waves. I'm sure many people that day looked at their need of Jesus in a different way after that encounter.

The same appearance of the glory has occured to me in ministry several times since then. The Lord is going to increase His visitations this way in these latter days.

When I was about 25 years old, I went out for a coffee with my friends brother. The plan was that I would share the Gospel of Christ with him. As soon as we sat down the Holy Ghost was speaking to me what to tell Brad. I said, "Brad, the Holy Ghost is telling me to be very bold with you about the Gospel of Christ. I'm going to be as bold with you about Christ as your friends are at work when they invite you to go out and party." I continued with similar words for a couple of minutes and then said to him, "The Holy Ghost wants to live in you and reveal Jesus Christ to you as your Lord and Savior." As I was saying these words to him, suddenly the glory of the Lord appeared in the air between us about one foot above the table! I stopped speaking and we couldn't even see each other through it! It appeared like living water just as when I was in the gymnasium, except this time it didn't fill the room. This time it was only a round patch about two feet in diameter. It was suspended in the air between us for about 60 seconds. Tears came to our eyes and I led Brad in a recommittment prayer to make Jesus His Lord and Savior.

What Do Signs Do?

They cause people to wonder and marvel at the awesome power of God and help them to open up to the possibility of something more. When the man who had the legion of devils was delivered by the Lord, they washed him up and clothed him. Jesus then sent him back to tell his friends what the Lord had done. He was so blessed by what the Lord had done, that he not only went back to his friends, but to the entire region! He went from city to city and village to village and when the Lord had returned the people in that same city were waiting expectantly for Him to bring a touch to them! The woman with the issue of blood was waiting for him. Jairus was there waiting for His return! There were crowds surrounding Him as soon as He returned. When the man came back, all the people marvelled at what the Lord had done for the man.

Mark 5:19-20
"Howbeit Jesus suffered him not, but saith unto him, Go home to thy friends, and tell them how great things the Lord hath done for thee, and hath had compassion on thee. And he departed, and began to publish in Decapolis how great things Jesus had done for him: and all *men* did marvel."

John 5:20
"For the Father loveth the Son, and sheweth him all things that himself doeth: and he will shew him greater works than these, that ye may marvel."

Matthew 9:6-8
"But that ye may know that the Son of man hath power on earth to forgive sins, (then saith he to the sick of the palsy,) Arise, take up thy bed, and go unto thine house. And he arose, and departed to his house.

But when the multitudes saw *it,* they marvelled, and glorified God, which had given such power unto men."

Matthew 9:33 "And when the devil was cast out, the dumb spake: and the multitudes marvelled, saying, It was never so seen in Israel."

The Day Of Pentecost

The Day of Pentecost as described in the book of Acts gives us a clear description of what happens when the Holy Ghost is poured out.

Acts 2:1-4
"And when the day of Pentecost was fully come, they were all with one accord in one place. And suddenly there came a sound from heaven as of a rushing mighty wind, and it filled all the house where they were sitting. And there appeared unto them cloven tongues like as of fire, and it sat upon each of them. And they were all filled with the Holy Ghost, and began to speak with other tongues, as the Spirit gave them utterance."

Pentecost Continued:

Acts 2:16-19
"But this is that which was spoken by the prophet Joel; And it shall come to pass in the last days, saith God, I will pour out of my Spirit upon all flesh: and your sons and your daughters shall prophesy, and your young men shall see visions, and your old men shall dream dreams: And on my servants and on my handmaidens I will pour out in those days of my Spirit; and they shall prophesy: And I will shew wonders in heaven above, and signs in the earth beneath; blood, and fire, and vapour of smoke…"

The outpouring of the Holy Ghost in this manner is a true Sign that the Holy Ghost has been given liberty in any place where we gather together in His name. Where these things are not happening, it's because He has not been given liberty. These are the true signs of the true Body of Christ. Where He is, there's always these things happening. The Day of Pentecost was not a one day event. It was the beginning of a new age where the Lord is pouring out His glory upon all flesh and it's poured out through His people. We then give the people the Good News and lead them to take Jesus Christ of Nazareth as their Lord and their Savior. That will then lead to a chain of events in their lives that will transform them into the image of Christ and then they can go and do the same things that Jesus did. (See John 14:12 & 20:21) Jesus is not dead and He's not just standing on the outside looking in. When we gather in His name, He's there and ready to pour out His Spirit through us all the time. We just need to believe it. Do we really believe or are we just waiting and hoping that one day He will come visit us with power after we have prayed enough? No amount of prayer will convince Him to do what He already promised to do.

Guard The Word In Your Heart

Read the Word and get the understanding from the Holy Ghost. It's when we hear the word of the kingdom and don't understand it, that the devil will come to take that Word Seed away. Look at the Words of Jesus:

Matthew 13:19
"When any one heareth the word of the kingdom, and understandeth *it* not, then cometh the wicked *one,* and catcheth away that which was sown in his heart. This is he which received seed by the way side."

A Rushing Mighty Wind

Chapter 4

Before I share my story with you about the Pentecostal Wind that was blowing, I want to share with you a scripture from the book of Acts about it. The Word is always the best place to begin. It always proceeds revelation which always proceeds the gift of faith. Faith comes from the revelation of The Word.

Acts 2:1-4 "And when the day of Pentecost was fully come, they were all with one accord in one place. And suddenly there came a sound from heaven as of a rushing mighty wind, and it filled all the house where they were sitting. And there appeared unto them cloven tongues like as of fire, and it sat upon each of them. And they were all filled with the Holy Ghost, and began to speak with other tongues, as the Spirit gave them utterance."

I personally love this part of the Bible more than any other. It's the Father's promise of the Holy Ghost coming from Heaven to earth. It's the invasion of the glory of God, and with a BANG!!! "I was once blind, but now I see the glory of the Lord!" This is what comes to mind when I read this portion of scripture. Jesus said that the kingdom comes not with observation, but what we see here is not the coming of the kingdom of God, for it was already here. The kingdom was already at hand, but now, it was not only at hand, but within the Believers in Christ, just as He had told them.

The word kingdom, means, "royalty" first and "realm" second. We fit into both aspects of the kingdom of God. We ARE the "royal priesthood" and we ARE "seated in heavenly places with Christ Jesus." We ARE the priests of a New Biblical Age AND Covenant. The Levitical Priesthood of the law was dissolved through Christ's death and resurrection, thus making them invalid. There was no more animal sacrifices! There was no more need for the tabernacle made with hands! There's now a New Priesthood! We are not like them, operating in the natural, visible tabernacle, but rather, we ARE the tabernacle and we ARE OF the realm that is invisible to natural eyes. That's the kingdom within us that's unseen to the eyes of this world. They see us and they see the glory of God on us, because it's radiating out of us. We are different, because we ARE different in every aspect of the word. We are saturated with the glory of God. We are temples of God Himself with the fullness of the Godhead is in us. Now, it may seem that I'm digressing, but this is all essential spiritual knowledge that must proceed what you are about to read. In fact, I would suggest reading this carefully before proceeding. Spiritual activity takes place through the planting of the Word of God into our spirit, so prepare yourself thoroughly to receive the revelation of the Word of God as by the Holy Ghost, the Revealer of the Word. I am NOT the revealer of the Word of God, I am your brother, and am sharing with you what He has given me to share, for the purpose of assisting you in discovering how to hear from Him yourself regarding His Word. The Holy Ghost is the one who guides us into all truth. I can only give you a shadow of the revelation that He has given me. You can only receive the fullness of it through Him. All day, I have many revelations running through my mind just like blood continually runs through my veins. All day I am thinking of more that I wish I could add to this book, but that would require a multitude of volumes. What I want for you to learn, is how to hear from Him yourself, if you haven't already done so. Once you learn to hear from Him yourself, then you will have some personal gems to impart to others. We should never rely on the revelation that another person has received. The revelation of others have been great catalysts for me, but never enough for me. I needed to take what I learned from them and dig in deeper for myself.

Ok, back to Acts 2. The word for "wind" in the Greek, has a meaning that will blow your mind sky high, but you have to be ready for it. Are you ready? I mean, are you open? Take a second and make sure you're really open, because you don't want to miss this. Ok, here it is. The word "wind" in the Greek, as used here in Acts chapter 2, means: "breath of life". Can you say, "Wow!" I don't know about you, but as soon as I think of that, all kinds of scriptures come to my mind. The first one that comes to mind, is Genesis 2:7, which says, "And the LORD God formed man *of* the dust of the ground, and breathed into his nostrils the breath of life; and man became a living soul."

"Listen carefully" was what the Lord said to me on the mountain side in 1987. Jesus came to restore to mankind what was lost in the Garden of Eden. He came to BRING BACK the "Breath of Life"! That's what the day of Pentecost was all about! It was, and IS God coming to dwell with and IN mankind. He died on the cross of Calvary to pay for the sins of all mankind, including Adams sin, so that He could legally restore all that was lost in the Garden, and thus He stripped Satan of all that he had stolen through Adams sin. After Adam sinned, the LORD had him do an animal sacrifice for the pardon of him and Eve's sin, and the skin of the animal that was sacrificed was used as clothing to cover their nakedness. That animal sacrifice was fulfilled in Christ, who came as "the Lamb of God who taketh away the sins of the world." He came to fulfill the law, including all the sacrifices made by the animals for the sins of all people. Every animal sacrifice that was ever made by God's leading was a temporary sacrifice that could only be fulfilled through Christ. The blood of animals could not remove sin, but only bring forgiveness of sins done. The sins still needed to be removed and they were removed through Christ. (See John 1:29 my favorite scripture when preaching in China)

That's why Jesus went to preach to those who were in Abraham's bosom (paradise).

Luke 23:42-43 "And he said unto Jesus, Lord, remember me when thou comest into thy kingdom. And Jesus said unto him, Verily I say unto thee, To day shalt thou be with me in paradise."

Luke 16:22 "And it came to pass, that the beggar died, and was carried by the angels into Abraham's bosom: the rich man also died, and was buried."

Jesus prophesied that the dead would hear His voice, saying, **John 5:25** "Verily, verily, I say unto you, The hour is coming, and now is, when the dead shall hear the voice of the Son of God: and they that hear shall live."

Matthew 27:50-53 "Jesus, when he had cried again with a loud voice, yielded up the ghost. And, behold, the veil of the temple was rent in twain from the top to the bottom; and the earth did quake, and the rocks rent; and the graves were opened; and many bodies of the saints which slept arose, and came out of the graves after his resurrection, and went into the holy city, and appeared unto many."

He preached the Good News of Christ to them, how He came as the Messiah to fulfill all the law and the prophets so that they could receive the redemption they had been waiting hundreds of years for. As a result, many Old Testament saints raised from the dead to give a witness to the Messiah. Oh, how I wish I could digress and spend a lot of time talking about that one event alone! What a revelation! I think I could write an entire book about the death and resurrection of Christ and maybe one day I will. What an Awesome God!

It was October 28th, 2010. I had been living in China for about 6 months. When I woke up that morning, I felt so awake and refreshed as though I had been awake for several hours already. I had never felt that way upon waking up while living in China, because the bed's I slept on were hard, and I am not used to that. Normally when I woke up, it took me at least two hours to feel clear minded.

I sat up on my bed with my back against the wall and said to the Lord, "Lord, what is it that you are wanting to do. I know you are wanting to do something, because I never felt this way upon waking up in the morning." I lifted my hands towards Heaven, and suddenly a rushing mighty wind began blowing upon me from Heaven. It was coming from above me. At that moment I knew that the Lord was pouring out

His promised Holy Spirit upon me in the same way He did when I was about to jump off a mountain cliff edge in 1987.

I made sure that all my windows were closed and stayed in my home for the rest of the day. The rushing mighty wind never stopped all day. It felt as though there was an electric fan directly over my head blowing upon me. The feeling was that of a cool wind that brought refreshing. I knew that the Lord was increasing the overflow of His Kingdom on earth as it is in Heaven. Joy flooded my soul and I was smiling the whole day.

The next day my translator called me at about 4:30pm. She said that she felt like the Lord was asking her to invite me to the Bible study in her house that night and if I would give a message. I agreed and went outside to immediately catch a taxi to get there.

The Bible study began one hour later. After I got out of the taxi and met my translator, I had a strong feeling that the Lord had a Divine plan for that nights Bible study.

There was a small group of people in the meeting that night of about 12 people, three of whom were non-believers. One of them was my translators mother and two others that had been invited that night for the first time. There was a time of praise and worship and then I was introduced and welcomed to share with the people, when suddenly the wind of the Holy Ghost began blowing in the room! I asked the people how many were feeling the wind in the room. Every person was feeling it. I then said, "I'm not going to share a message tonight, because the Lord is ready to do something already. Let's just continue praising Him until He shows us what He's doing."

As we continued praising the Lord told me to ask who there needed healing. Three people put their hand up. One was my translators mother, one was another one of the three unbelievers and the other was the translators sister. The mother said she has diabetes. I stretched my hand towards her and commanded that diabetic spirit to leave her and she began to shake a little for about 10 seconds then she shouted and the look of fear was briefly on her face. She then began to smile and told us what happened.

When I commanded the spirit to leave, she felt it struggling inside her and it felt dark and evil to her. She never felt that before and it scared her and so she screamed, but then she felt it leave her body through the top of her head and she then felt peace come upon her, and she knew she was now free. She became a believer in Jesus that night. She also became a ministry team member for the next 8 months until I flew back to Canada.

One day, very shortly after her mother was saved, my translator had come to eat lunch with her. When she walked in the apartment, she was surprised to see two women on their knees and her mother with them leading them in the prayer for salvation. She said that the Lord told her to go to her two neighbors and invite them for tea because she had something very important to tell them but she was afraid because she told the Lord she was still a babies and didn't know what to tell her neighbors. The Lord reassured her that He would tell her what to tell them. The result was that these two women were saved. When the women had come over, she shared with them the Good News of Christ and then asked them if she could lay hands on them to be healed. She explained to them that healing was a part of the salvation that Jesus died for. They agreed and we're instantly healed of their conditions and then they got on their knees and raised their hands up high to the Lord and said a prayer for salvation.

The other woman, who was an unbeliever as well and was in attendance to thus Bible study, had one collapsed lung. I stretched forth my hand to her and had my translator lay hands on her. The woman began weeping heavily and she felt air fill her lung. That caused her to weep even more. She felt so loved by the Lord. She happily said the prayer for salvation and accepted Jesus as her Lord and Savior. She was totally healed. All glory to God.

What is the wind? It's the air of Heaven. It's Heaven coming on earth. It's an invisible open portal that's releasing the very breath of God upon the earth. It's the promised Holy Spirit that Jesus sent from Heaven after His resurrection. It's His Kingdom come on earth as it is in Heaven.

Acts 2:1-4

"And when the day of Pentecost was fully come, they were all with one accord in one place. **And suddenly there came a sound from heaven as of a rushing mighty wind, and it filled all the house where they were sitting.** And there appeared unto them cloven tongues like as of fire, and it sat upon each of them. And they were all filled with the Holy Ghost, and began to speak with other tongues, as the Spirit gave them utterance."

When the wind is blowing, it brings comfort. I like to call it "the soft presence of the Lord". It brings tremendous peace and comfort to our soul. We even feel physical peace in our bodies beyond any pharmaceutical sedative.

The wind is the comfort of Heaven experienced on earth. The way we will feel when we are in Heaven, is the way that the wind of the Holy Spirit makes us feel on earth. Anxieties dissipate. Sorrows are resolved. Grief's become a thing of the past. When I am feeling anxious about any issue in my life, I get in a position that will help me to open myself up to His Presence; and as I do, I feel the peace that passes all understanding come upon me and I no longer feel anxious. I feel His comfort because of His grace which is easily accessible in His glory. (See 2Corinthians 3:17 & Hebrews 4:16) The wind is His glory being poured out into the earth, until one day it will fill the earth as the waters cover the sea.

I liken it to being sedated just prior to having surgery done or having a tooth pulled. I have experienced this several times. Once for having my wisdom teeth extracted, and 5 other times for having 5 molar teeth extracted at different times in my life. The moment that the drug kicks in, you feel yourself feeling no care about anything.

From that day, when the wind began blowing upon me on October 28, 2010, until now, the same rushing mighty wind blows in every meeting where I'm preaching.

What happens when I'm preaching, is that I will feel the wind blowing and I will ask how many people are feeling it. The Lord uses it sometimes to reveal to me people who aren't saved or simply need a miracle. For example: I remember the third meeting after the wind began. It was in my large living room where we comfortably set up about 45 plastic stools which were all occupied. Just after I started preaching I felt the wind on my left cheek. I then said, "How many people just felt a very cool wind on their left cheek? Three hands raised up. It turned out that all those three people were unbelievers and that day the Lord touched them by His Holy Spirit Pentecostal wind as a Sign and Wonder of Him. The other thing about that was that those three people had come together so when they all raised their hands it must have registered in their minds that, out of the 45 people present, it was no coincidence that only they felt it on their cheeks at the same time.

Jesus said that the Holy Spirit would convict the world of sin, righteousness and judgment. It's no doubt that this ministry of the Holy Spirit is an integral part of redemption for lost souls. (See John 16:8-11 & Acts 2:37-40)

He never sends us alone to share the Gospel of Christ. He equips us with The Holy Ghost and Power to confirm His Word as we deliver it to the people.

1Corinthians 2:4-5 "And my speech and my preaching was not with enticing words of man's wisdom, but in demonstration of the Spirit and of power: That your faith should not stand in the wisdom of men, but in the power of God."

It brings refreshing, renewal, healing and restoration in body, heart, mind and soul. There are no extravagant words needed when He shows up this way. His glory does it all. His arms His Words with Signs following as they are shared. People all over the room will begin getting words and suddenly feel bold enough to lay hands on others to be healed. They begin getting words of knowledge. I have seen this happen again and again. The wind fills the room and everyone feels it. The people begin flowing in it just like swimming down a river.

I remember preaching in one church while I was still in Canada, where I just spoke out three words of knowledge that the Lord had given me and they were all correct. The three people were instantly healed and then everyone in the church gathered around them joyfully asking them how it felt when they were healed. As the three that were healed were giving testimony about their experience, the wind blew through the whole room and everyone started to get healed instantly. Then laughter broke out amongst us all for several minutes. It was the glory of Heaven filling the room and filling us. "Joy unspeakable and full of glory." We were experiencing the glory of Heaven on earth.

He said that where two or three are gathered together in His name He would be present. (See Matthew 18:20) I had pressed into the Kingdom of God, expecting this reality just as I had read it in the New Testament, and He confirmed every word, and continues to do so in my life today. But not just for me! For others also. I discovered that the Chinese people were able to step into this outpouring of the Holy Spirit very quickly. They were very hungry for the glory of the Lord and pressed in for it.

I invited the people to share testimonies every week. The stories were astounding. One woman was sharing Jesus everywhere she went and was leading at the least one person to Jesus every day. Another woman, who was already retired, was sharing Jesus all day and praying for people and they were being touched and healed. One young man, who was attending high school still, prayed for a friend at school who had a twisted arm and he was instantly healed in front of another friend. They were shocked at the miracle that happened in front of their own eyes.

The people who were attending my meetings always felt inspired to share their testimonies at their home church each week. They would keep getting up to share another testimony until the pastor had to finally cut them off because it took up so much time. They laughed, they cried, they shouted praises to God for all the Good things He was doing in their midst. As a result, Jesus was becoming very famous amongst them and when friends and family heard of the testimonies, they would come to see for themselves, and they were never disappointed. Churches were multiplying in size with the new Believers they were bringing.

Does The Wind Only Blow In China?

The wind of the Holy Spirit blew irregularly when I was doing ministry in Canada and the USA. It wasn't until October 28, 2010 that it became a common manifestation of the Holy Spirit in my ministry. Now it happens every time I do ministry, even while in Canada. I can be with one or two people just talking about Jesus in a coffee shop and it will blow. It normally comes as a cool gentle breeze, like refreshing air conditioning.

One friend from church was with me for coffee for the first time, and as I was talking about Jesus, I felt the wind begin blowing and asked him if he felt it. His eyes got big, and he said, "Yes!" He was amazed! He had thought it was maybe just one of my experiences overseas in China. About two weeks later, he was feeling very sick and was missing work because of it, so he decided to have a very hot bath. While sitting in the bath, he felt the cool wind of the Holy Spirit come over him and immediately in his mind, he knew it was the Holy Spirit, because he had no where for a wind to come from in his washroom. He felt the glory fill him, and his face began to shine, and his symptoms dissipated immediately leaving him feeling well.

The Holy Ghost came as a representative of Christ on earth so that He can be everywhere at the same time and administer the fullness of the Gospel of Christ around the entire globe simultaneously.

We don't see where the wind comes from, because it's coming from an invisible doorway in the heavenly places in Christ. (See Ephesians 2:4) That's the Kingdom of God/Heaven on earth now. Jesus preached it was here now and it is. He is the door and it's through Him that we enter into the Heavenly Places where we are seated together with Christ. (See John 10:7-9) Heaven continually invades earth in our midst and most of us never recognize it when it does. It's when we become more educated on it that we become more conscious of it in our daily lives.

The Kingdom of God that Jesus and His Disciples Preached:

Mark 1:14-15
"Jesus came into Galilee, **preaching the gospel of the kingdom of God,** And saying, The time is fulfilled, and the kingdom of God is at hand: repent ye, and believe the gospel."

Matthew 9:35
"And Jesus went about all the cities and villages, teaching in their synagogues, and **preaching the gospel of the kingdom,** and healing every sickness and every disease among the people."

Matthew 4:16-17
"The people which sat in darkness saw great light; and to them which sat in the region and shadow of death light is sprung up. From that time Jesus began to preach, and to say, Repent: for **the kingdom of heaven is at hand."**

Luke 4:43
"And he said unto them, **I must preach the kingdom of God to other cities also:** for therefore am I sent."

Luke 9:1-2
"Then he called his twelve disciples together, and gave them power and authority over all devils, and to cure diseases. And he sent them to **preach the kingdom of God,** and to heal the sick."

Luke 9:59-60
"And he said unto another, Follow me. But he said, Lord, suffer me first to go and bury my father. Jesus said unto him, Let the dead bury their dead: but go thou and **preach the kingdom of God."**

Matthew 10:7-8
"And as ye go, **preach, saying, The kingdom of heaven is at hand.** Heal the sick, cleanse the lepers, raise the dead, cast out devils: freely ye have received, freely give."

CLOTHED WITH INVISIBLE CLOTHING

Isaiah 61:10
"I will greatly rejoice in the LORD, my soul shall be joyful in my God; for **he hath clothed me with the garments of salvation (Heb. Liberty, deliverance, prosperity), he hath covered me with the robe of righteousness (Heb. (In government) of Judge, ruler, king),** as a bridegroom decketh *himself* with ornaments, and as a bride adorneth *herself* with her jewels."

Psalm 132:9
"Let thy priests be clothed with righteousness (Heb. Justice, rightness); and let they saints shout for joy."

Revelation 1:5B-6A
"Unto him that loved us, and washed us from our sins in his own blood, And hath made us kings and priests unto God and his Father; to him be glory and dominion for ever and ever. Amen."

1Peter 2:9-10
"But ye are a chosen generation, a royal priesthood, an holy nation, a peculiar people; that ye should shew forth the praises of him who hath called you out of darkness into his marvelous light: Which in time past were not a people, but are now the people of God: which had not obtained mercy, but now have obtained mercy."

The priesthood of the Old Testament was a type and shadow of the New Testament priesthood. They wore different garments for different services. (See Ezekiel 42:14). The Lord has made us kings and priests unto God and His Father. As priests we have been clothed upon with the suitable garments as given by the Lord Jesus Himself to us, just as He had them made for the priesthood of the Old Testament. Each garment signifies a form of ministry. There are garments of power for the royal priesthood after the order of Melchisidec, which is a kingly priesthood. This garment holds the authority and power of the fullness of the God head. Jesus walked in it as the King of kings and has clothed his kings with it.

The priests of the Old Testament were given natural garments made with hands. We who are the royal priesthood of the New Testament have been given spiritual garments not made with the hands of men. The garments that the priesthood wore in the holy place were holy and were not to be worn in the utter court. We, as the royal priesthood of the Lord are clothed upon with holy garments of righteousness for ministry and thereby enter into the holy places through Jesus Christ who is the door. (See Ezekiel 42:14)

The priesthood of the O.T. had governmental authority in the nation of Israel. The priesthood of the Church of Jesus Christ carries with it tremendous authority in the spirit and through that has powerful authority on earth to bless the people and the land. We have the power and authority of the name Jesus to release spiritual blessings that will bring health and healing not only to people, but to bring forth bumper crops. We have authority and power over the elements, including water, wind and fire. Jesus demonstrated that His authority and power can operate through human flesh and then He made the boldest statement, saying that we who believe can do all the same things that He did. (See John 14:12) He even went as far as to say that we would do even greater things. Does that include walking on water? Why not? He did it. I haven't done it, but I believe that with God all things are possible. If walking on water would help provide proof to His existence for the non-believers, then so be it. If my walking on water in His name would help them to listen openly to the Gospel of Christ, then I would walk on water for that.

It's time for His Believers to stand up and take the challenge to believe what Jesus said we could do and go do it. If we don't, He will raise up a New Generation that will and we will be left behind. We need to get out of our church rut and go beyond those four walls and do something for the Gospel of Christ. We don't need permission. Jesus gave it to us already and He said that He would be with us til the end of the world, so we can know that we are never alone. (See Matthew 28:18-20) We don't need anyone else to approve for us what He commanded us to do.

The garment of linen and linen breeches for the burnt offering: See Leviticus 6:10

When I was a new believer, I had great faith to see the glory of the Lord. I was always excited to be with Him. He showed me Heaven and a multitude of believers all dressed in white worshipping Jesus. Jesus was preaching to them and I was up close to Him. I had been sitting on my door step in the warmth of the sun on one of my days off when it happened. I was reading my Bible when suddenly I heard a man's voice preaching. I closed my eyes and began to pray because I didn't know where the voice was coming from. Then suddenly I was lifted into Heaven where I was up high with Him at His throne. I was about 20 years old at the time.

I listened to Him preach in His deep bass like voice but I couldn't understand the language He was preaching in. He would stop preaching every 60 seconds or so, and when He did, the millions of hands would raise up simultaneously and shout praises to Him. Then all hands would simultaneously lower and He would begin preaching again. This continued for at least 10 minutes where there was an exchange of preaching and praises. Then suddenly I was with open eyes back at my doorstep. I have had many visions or call them visitations since that time, but not without ridicule and scrutiny from Modern-Day-Believers. I call them Modern-Day-Believers, because they don't resemble the Believers of the early church believers at all. They have a form of godliness but deny the power thereof. I consider them to be intruders. They are not of the body of Christ. (See 2Timothy 3:5) They argue and dispute the activity of the Word of God, accusing and resisting the truth as though Jesus is no longer active in the earth. What will they do when Jesus appears in clouds of His glory to take us home in our resurrected bodies? They may say He's the antichrist because it doesn't sit right with their doctrines and they will be the ones left behind.

Jesus said:

Matthew 5:20
"For I say unto you, That except your righteousness (Gr. innocence) shall exceed *the righteousness* of the scribes and Pharisees, ye shall in no case enter into the kingdom of heaven."

How can we enter into the Kingdom of Heaven unless we exceed the righteousness (innocence) of the scribes and Pharisees? First of all, we must be Born Again.

John 3:3, 5
"Jesus answered and said unto him, Verily, verily, I say unto thee, Except a man be born again, he cannot see the kingdom of God... Jesus answered, Verily, verily, I say unto thee, Except a man be born of water and *of* the Spirit, he cannot enter into the kingdom of God."

Once we are Born Again, by grace, through faith in the atoning sacrifice of Jesus Christ, we receive access into the Kingdom of God. (The Kingdom of God and the Kingdom of Heaven are the same thing.) He is the door and we enter in and out through Him. Hopefully we will spend more time in than out.

A garment of salvation and a robe of righteousness is placed upon us, and though we are not yet perfect, (we know that) we are washed clean by the blood of the Lamb and clothed with white clothing. If we make faults, and we do, our clothing still covers us. Our sins are continually removed as we continually go before the Lord and ask forgiveness of our daily sins and ask Him to wash us in His blood from them all. (See 1John 1:7 "And the blood of Jesus Christ his Son cleanseth us from all sin.") Our garments are washed clean, and wrinkles removed.

Let's look at more verses regarding the righteousness (Gr. Innocence) that's by grace through faith. As we read these verses, keep in mind that we were once sinners, but now, by the blood of Jesus Christ, we have been made innocent before God. We can now come boldly unto the throne of grace, just as if we never sinned, because we are clothed upon with garments of righteousness. (See Hebrews 4:16) That's the meaning of our justification in Christ. Our sins have been cast as far as the east is from the west. (See Psalm 103:12) We may remember them and the devil may remember them and remind us of them, but He has forgotten them and that's all that matters.

Romans 3:21-22
"But now the righteousness (innocence) of God without the law is manifested, being witnessed by the law and the prophets; **Even the righteousness (innocence) of God *which is* by faith of Jesus Christ unto all and upon all them that believe."**

Paul says to the Romans, that the righteousness is unto all and UPON all them that believe. He didn't say that it's only to the priest of the church or the minister, deacon or elder. It's not for some elite members in the church. It's to ALL THEM THAT BELIEVE. Once we included ourselves in the group of sinners, but now we can include ourselves in the group of the righteous. We were once carnal, but have now put off the old man and put on the new. If we don't feel righteous, it may be because we don't understand the Word of God and all that Jesus accomplished for us on the cross. We are NEW CREATURES in Christ. Old things have passed away. We still live in a flesh temple, but we are not the temple. We live in it, but, we are meant to follow the Holy Ghost, not the temple of the Holy Ghost.

The priesthood is not for those who get educated in Bible School and get a man made certificate that calls them an ordained priest of pastor. That's man's idea. The priesthood is for all believers. Everyone of us are a part of the royal priesthood. As long as we think that only those educated and ordained by men are qualified to have the move of the Holy Ghost in their lives, they will continually come short of the glory of God. The man made ordination is just smoke and mirrors. That ordination doesn't qualify them to be used by the Holy Ghost. The salvation that brings about the kingly royal priesthood for the Gospel of Christ is the only ordination that qualifies us.

I had the ordination card and papers before. Guess what? They didn't make my ministry more effective for the salvation of souls. I threw them out about 15 years ago.

See more verses about righteousness at the end of the chapter.

Where in any of the four Gospels did Jesus ever discuss any kind of man made ordination to qualify believers to do what He did? He said, Mark 16:17-20 "And these signs shall follow them that believe; In my name shall they cast out devils; they shall lay hands on the sick and they shall recover."

Jesus said:

Acts 1:8
"But ye shall receive power, after that the Holy Ghost is come upon you: and ye shall be witnesses."
Luke 24:49
"And, behold, I send the promise of my Father upon you: but tarry ye in the city of Jerusalem, until ye be **endued with power from on high.**"

The Greek meaning for the word **"endued",** as used in Luke 24:49 means: "(in the sense of sinking into a garment); to invest with clothing (literally or figuratively): - array, clothe (with), endue, have (put) on.)"

That robe of righteousness becomes endued with power and authority once we are baptized with the Holy Ghost and Fire. Its like pouring gasoline over a vesture and lighting it on fire with a lighter.

I still remember in the mid 90's when I had my first encounters with the baptism of fire. I remember being at my friends house and physically feeling flames of fire touch me as he walked past me during a house meeting in his home. We become saturated with the contagious anointing of the glory and Power of the Holy Ghost. (See Acts 1:8, 10:38 & John 20:21)(1John 4:17 "Because as he is so are we in this world." Notice that it says, "As he is", not "As he was.") Now we are as He is. How is He now? He is clothed with glory and the kingly-priesthood robe of righteousness. Jesus, when praying to the Heavenly Father said:

"And the glory which thou gavest me I have given them; that they may be one, even as we are one." (See John 17:22)

As soon as you leave your house, the public devils see the glory radiating from you and they are shaking in their shoes. They are very afraid of us. They know the power of the glory of the Holy Ghost that we are clothed with. They see the burning glory that rests on us. They are not stupid. They know that we overpower them by this kingly-priesthood glory. There's no need to be afraid of the devil. Jesus overcame him and all his tricks and He gave us power over all the power of the devil to tread on serpents and scorpions. He sends us to cast out devils. How can we do that if we are afraid of them? They are afraid of us. They know we have the name of Jesus and are clothed in His glory. They know that we are not alone better than most of us do because we've been counseled to be afraid of the devil lest he harm us. The devil has deceived many Modern-Believers into thinking that the devil is dangerous to us. We are dangerous to him!

Is It Hard To Be Clothed Upon With Power?

Against all popular belief that it's very difficult to get this anointing of the Holy Ghost, I must say, it's not difficult at all. He wants to clothe us with His power and authority but in order to have it and walk in it, we need to shake off the contradictory lies we've been told.

He said that the labourers are few, so we should pray for more of them for the harvest is ripe and ready for picking. (See Luke 10:2) It means that there's no shortage of work in the Kingdom of God and there's no shortage of power to do it. The only shortage we have, is Strong Believers who like to eat meat and not just milk. Strong meat is for the doers of the Word of God. Milk is for babies that can't do anything. Jesus said, "My meat is to do the will of him that sent me, and to finish his work." (See John 4:34) (Also see James 1:22-25 "But be ye doers of the word, and not hearers only, deceiving your own selves." Verse 25 says: "but a doer of the work, this man shall be blessed in his deed."

This is not inferring that a person must serve in the church. It's referring to putting action to our faith that comes from hearing the Word of God.

This can include work in the church, but is not defined by doing work in the church. We apply the Word of God to every realm of our lives outside of the church and then after that we can apply it to our life in the church. Its application should always begin in our own personal lives with our families, work places, friends and associates.

Maybe most of us don't feel the call to do a ministry outside of our family life. That's fine, because family life is a mission field in itself and a worthy ministry. If we are called to do more, the Lord will call us and we will know. Regardless, the fact remains that we are a shining light to all those who come into contact with us, whether in our family, work place or just walking through the grocery store. The first person I remember blessing me with the message of the gospel was my hair dresser. He didn't even say much about it, but there was something about the man that I was drawn to. He had a small Bible on his counter with all his scissors and such and I asked him what it was. When he told me I said, "Oh you don't really believe in God do you?" His response was simply, saying, "I believe in God and I believe that He helps me in my life." That was all he said, but I was drawn to something about him and I couldn't put my finger on it. I wish he had felt to share more with me at that time, nonetheless, it was a gospel seed planted into my heart and the Lord saved me about 6 months later.

The First Time I Saw The Robe Of Righteousness On Me:

The first time I visibly saw the robe of righteousness upon me, was when I was in prayer on my knees in my bedroom in about 1989. I was in a white room that had no walls and I could see the floor continue for as far as my eyes could see. I was kneeling on the floor beside an angel, and our elbows were leaning upon a small wooden white bench. We prayed there for about 7 hours. I had been in prayer on my bed that night and as soon as I put my head on my pillow, I was taken into this vision. We were praying in the gift of tongues and it seemed we were doing warfare. I was wearing a long white robe that was very soft. I didn't understand that it was a robe of righteousness until May 2011 while I was doing ministry in China. When in China, one day when I was on my knees in prayer in my bedroom, Jesus appeared before me, or should I say, my eyes were opened to see Him there before me. He was dancing elegantly. His robe was floating on Him and it was dancing with Him as He moved in circles, waving His arms in the most lovely motions. At that very moment, my eyes were opened to see the robe of righteousness that I have been clothed with. It looked a lot like the one He was wearing. It was floating over my skin and seemed to be alive. There was light glistening from it and clouds of glory all around it.

Just as the wind came on March 28th, 2010 and remained all that day, so was the visibility of the robe upon me. I could see and feel it all day, but not only all day. I could see and feel it all week almost all day long. I was seeing with my spiritual eyes and natural eyes at the same time. It was fantastic! The robe of righteousness is alive! I was used to receiving ministry from the Lord all the time, but now I saw the source of the glory and power that was upon me. It's the glory and power of the Lord that was in and upon the robe of righteousness. We are so blessed! Whenever I think about the robe upon me and how it looks, I feel the joy of the Lord and the glory begins to shine upon my face.

The week that I saw the robe floating upon me was about two weeks before I was to return to Canada. It was the same week that my team and I were invited to do ministry in some larger churches in a city that was about three hours drive from where we were. When we went to this city, my spiritual eyes were opened again and I saw it on me the entire time I was preaching. It was an awesome experience! The robe wasn't me. It was Him on me. I knew everything I needed to do more clearly than ever before. Seeing it and knowing it was Him on me caused a greater boldness to flow from me in that meeting. I was feeling everything that was happening in the heavenly places. I hadn't felt it with such detail ever before. I knew everything that He was doing with ease and that made it easier to follow Him.

There was about 700 people in the first church I preached in that day. I literally felt the Holy Ghost fire dripping from my hands as I was on the stage preaching. I had just released 16 of my ministry team members to go into the crowd and lay hands on the people and pray for them. The crowd was excited and reaching for their hands to pray for them because of all the miracles they had just witnessed.

I began throwing my hands towards the crowd, as if I was trying to get water off my hands onto them. It wasn't water, it was the Holy Ghost fire power. As I was throwing my hands towards the crowd, the fire was falling all over them. My team members told me afterwards that they could feel the fire falling like rain as I did. They were feeling the empowerment of the Holy Ghost. They were scared at first, but once they went into the crowd of needy believers, they felt the boldness of the Holy Ghost and the people were getting healed quickly. They were busy until the time we had to go to the next church. Between the two churches where we ministered that day, there was about 45 testimonies of deaf ears and eyes opening. One woman who was paralyzed from the waist down began walking in front of the whole church. That was the point that the crowd went ballistic. They saw the woman walking and started running to me to pray for them. I had to run back to the stage to prevent myself from being crushed under them. That was when I sent the sixteen team members out to lay hands on all those needing a miracle.

I wish I had it on video. It was the most amazing demonstration of the Holy Ghost and power I had ever witnessed in my life. I know that the Lord is wanting to release this kind of demonstration of the His glory and power in His churches worldwide. He wants His church to evolve into the living organism that He created it to be and He's looking for volunteers globally. We are not living up to our potential as the Body of Christ on earth. We have the Kingdom of God inside of us, on us and in our midst as we gather in His name. The world should be running to us, not from us. We should be telling them the Good News, not the Bad News. John the Baptist was preaching against the peoples sins. Jesus only preached good news. He sent the Holy Ghost to convict the world of sin, righteousness and judgement. Jesus has prepared the way for us to continue doing all that He began. He gave us the example of how to spread the Good News. (See Acts 1:1) We need to copy Him, not John the Baptist. Jesus never preached bad news to the world. He only preached bad news to those who directly opposed Him. They were warned of the consequences of opposing Him. For the rest of the world, He showed His Love and mercy in the demonstration of the Holy Ghost and Power.

The Same Robe Of Righteousness As Was On Jesus:

I believe that this "Robe of Righteousness" that the Lord places upon us, is the same as the "Robe of Righteousness" that was witnessed upon Jesus by Peter, James and John on the mount of transfiguration. (Mark 9:1-3) It was glowing with the glory of God. Everywhere He went, the power of His riches in glory was flowing out of Him and all who touched Him by faith were in fact touching the "Robe of Righteousness" and that released the power of His riches in glory. (See Philippians 4:19, Ephesians 1:18 & Colossians 1:12)

They Saw Heaven On Earth:

I believe that when they saw Jesus on the mount of transfiguration, they were seeing the Kingdom of Heaven on earth. It's the invisible realms that our natural eyes and senses are naturally immune to. Nonetheless, I believe that this is the Kingdom of Heaven that's around us and active around us all the. Whenever I think about it, which is pretty often actually, I begin to feel my atmosphere being affected by it. When we think on the Kingdom of Heaven according to His Word, we are sowing spiritual seeds to reap a spiritual harvest in our lives. The outcome will be the overflow of the riches in His glory into our lives.

Mark 4:30-32
"And he said, Whereunto shall we liken the kingdom of God? or with what comparison shall we compare it? *It is* like a grain of mustard seed, which, when it is sown in the earth, is less than all the seeds that be in the earth: But when it is sown, it groweth up, and becometh greater than all herbs, and shooteth out great branches; so that the fowls of the air may lodge under the shadow of it."

I See Glory Clouds When I'm Preaching:

When I preach, I begin to see the glory clouds appear over the people and light is shining all around them. I am seeing with my spiritual eyes and natural eyes at the same time, just as Peter, James and John were seeing both when they saw Jesus on the mount of transfiguration and when they saw Him ascending into Heaven. I see

Jesus walking down the isle. When I say I see Jesus, I mean, I believe it's Him in our midst in spirit, not in the flesh, and occasionally He appears to individuals in the meetings. I believe that He's walking amongst us just as He said He would when two or three gather together in His name. (See Matthew 18:20) I believe that it's Him walking in our midst that's confirming the Word we preach with signs following. (See Mark 16:20) "the Lord working with them and confirming the word with signs following."

Philippians 4:5
"Let your moderation be known unto all men. The Lord *is* at hand."

Acts 11:21
"And the hand of the Lord was with them: and a great number believed, and turned unto the Lord."

Acts 13:11
"And now, behold, the hand of the Lord *is* upon thee, and thou shalt be blind, not seeing the sun for a season. And immediately there fell on him a mist and a darkness; and he went about seeking some to lead him by the hand."

Exodus 31:18
"And he gave unto Moses, when he had made an end of communing with him upon mount Sinai, two tables of testimony, tables of stone, written with the finger of God."

Luke 11:20
"But if I with the finger of God cast out devils, no doubt the kingdom of God is come upon you."

Jesus was clothed with invisible clothing. We know this is true according to His transfiguration on the mount. He didn't just put on some spiritual clothes for them to see that day. The Kingdom was upon Him just as a judge wears a robe that represents His authority and power. They were seeing what He looks like in the heavenly places on earth. There was invisible activity happening all around Him all the time.

Jesus makes an interesting statement in the book of John 3:12-13, saying, **"And no man hath ascended up to heaven, but he that came down from heaven, even the Son of man which is in heaven."** That's in the King James Version. "even the Son of man which is in heaven." How could He have been in Heaven while on earth at the same time? I thought He hadn't ascended until after His resurrection? It's because He was walking in the heavenly places on earth. It was His spirit that was walking in and aware of the heavenly places. His eyes were not dim due to sin. He could see in the spirit and natural realms at the same time. (See Isaiah 32:3 "And the eyes of them that see shall not be dim.") He was never separated from God because of sin. He had free access to the heavenly places and earth at the same time. He let Peter, James and John have a glimpse into what it looks like on the mount of transfiguration so that we could know about it. Few of us may actually get to see it, but at least we can know that we are walking in Heaven while we are on earth, just as Jesus was. We are in fact walking in Heavenly places in our spirit now. (See Ephesians 2:6 "And hath raised *us* up together, and made *us* sit together in heavenly *places* in Christ Jesus."

We Are Evolving In Our Understanding Of Who We Really Are In Christ:

From what the Lord told me on the mountain side in 1987, I know that there's a time coming when His church is going to know who they are more clearly as the time of His return approaches. We are evolving in our understanding of who we really are in Christ. We are changed into the image of the Lord, from glory to glory, by the Spirit of the Lord. (See 2Corinthians 3:18) There's one thing for sure and that's the fact that the devil is watching to see the progression of the Believers in Christ. It's a gauge for him to know the timeline that the Lord has set in place. The devil is doing all that he can to keep the Believers deceived of who they really are in Christ. He knows that once we wake up to the things of the spirit with eyes wide open, his time is short. He knows that once we truly know who we are, he's really in trouble.

Jesus made it clear that no man besides Himself had ever been in both places at once, but now that we are born again and seated in heavenly places with Christ, we are in fact, as Christ was, in Heaven on earth.

Moses, David, Abraham and other prophets of God were not walking in Heaven on earth before Christ. His church, which is His Body on earth, is walking in the Kingdom of Heaven on earth now. Some say that Enoch walked into Heaven in his flesh temple, but the Bible doesn't say or imply that at all. It just says that "Enoch walked with God: and he *was* not; for God took him." (See Genesis 5:24) I don't think that Enoch went to Heaven without his body dying. Others were spoken of as walking with God besides Enoch and they died. (See Genesis 6:9 "And Noah walked with God.")There's no mention of Enoch's burial, but I believe it means that his spirit left his body and went to be with the Lord and so it will be when our flesh dies, God will take our spirit to Heaven. Our flesh will go to the grave for a time until it's resurrected into new life by the glory of God.

We Become Hosts Of The Glory Of God:

There was so much spiritual activity happening around Him because of the glory that was shining from Him. He was hosting it. He was bringing it to the world and once it comes upon us, we become it's host. "Ye shall receive power, after that the Holy Ghost is come upon you." (See Acts 1:8) "What? know ye not that your body is the temple of the Holy Ghost *which is* in you, which ye have of God, and ye are not your own?" (See 1Corinthians 6:19)

The Purpose Of The Power Is To Be A Witness:

There's a purpose for that power. It's to be a witness of Jesus and His resurrection. "One must be ordained to be a witness with us of His resurrection." (See Acts 1:22)

Once His power comes upon us, we begin experiencing lots of spiritual activity happening around us. The clothing that He places upon us, enables us to walk in the heavenly places on earth as it is in Heaven.

We become walking power houses of the glory of God. It's radiating from us and all around us. People are getting touched by it's power and they don't even know it. Whenever there's a mighty outpouring of the Holy Ghost, people are affected by His Presence. They may be irritated because of the darkness that's in them or they may feel the peace that passes all understanding. I find that those who have more religion than faith are often irritated by the power of God in their midst and will attack it when they get the chance.

When we lay hands on those who are sick or diseased, we are releasing that power. We "Declare his glory among the heathen, his wonders among all people." (Psalm 96:3) Our spirit becomes "the candle of the LORD." (Proverbs 20:27) and Jesus said to "Let your light so shine before men, that they may see your good works, and glorify your Father which is in heaven." (See John 14:12 "He that believeth on me, the works that I do shall he do also." & Matthew 5:16) Peter clarifies the words of Jesus for us, saying, "But you are a chosen generation, a royal priesthood, an holy nation, a peculiar people; that ye should shew forth the praises of him who hath called you out of darkness into his marvellous light." (1Peter 2:9)

"The Spirit Of The Lord Is Upon Me":

Jesus said, "The Spirit of the Lord is upon me, because he hath anointed me to preach the gospel ..." (See Luke 4:18) By that Power, He gave demonstrations of the Spirit and of Power. "Jesus of Nazareth, a man approved of God among you by miracles and wonders and signs, which God did by him in the midst of you, as ye yourselves know." (See Acts 2:22) "How God anointed Jesus of Nazareth with the Holy Ghost and with power: who went about doing good, and healing all that were oppressed of the devil; for God was with him." (See Acts 10:38)

"The Kingdom Of God Is At Hand":

The Good News that Jesus was preaching was that "the Kingdom of God (See Mark 1:14-15 & Matthew 9:35) was at hand" and He sent the disciples to preach the same message. (See Matt. 10:7 & Luke 10:9) After His passion, they included in their message a witness of His resurrection.

I personally discovered that when preaching "the Kingdom of Heaven is at hand", and His resurrection, that miracles always happen. It's the message that Jesus preached and the message that He told His disciples to preach. If you want to see miracles, then study these two things and ask for a deep revelation of it. **In my opinion, these are the most important keys to seeing miracles occur in your ministry. It's no wonder they were in a mighty Holy Spirit outpouring for nearly 300 years after Christ rose from the dead and ascended to Heaven.** I make those two topics the main focus in every teaching lesson and miracle crusade message. It's the message that He always confirms with Signs following. That's what the Powers for. The Powers for a witness of His resurrection and His Kingdom at hand and within us.

Acts 4:33 "And with great power gave the apostles witness of the resurrection of the Lord Jesus: and great grace was upon them all." Great grace confirms the Word of the resurrection of the Lord Jesus.

"Verily I say unto you, That there be some of them that stand here, which shall not taste of death, till they have seen the kingdom of God come with power. ... he was transfigured before them. And his raiment became shining, exceeding white as snow; so as no fuller on earth can white them." (See Mk. 9:1-3)

His Appearance Is Arrayed With Glory:

Jesus can open our eyes to not only see how we look in the glory, but to see Him as He is in Glory. He can appear to us in a dream, vision or in His image by His Holy Spirit. Some claim that they may have seen Him in His flesh. We know that 500 plus people saw Him in His flesh soon after He resurrected from the grave and others later in years claimed to have seen Him in the flesh. Therefore, we know it's possible for Him to appear in His flesh and keep us from dying. It's the Glory that heals us from our diseases, sicknesses and ailments. We should not reject the glory by being afraid that it will kill our bodies. This is a lie of the devil to make us resistant to His Glory and Power. It brings correction to every part of our bodies. Just a little exposure to the Glory restores us in every realm of life. Too much exposure to the Glory will NOT destroy our flesh. If we are tired, depressed, oppressed or too stressed in our minds and emotions, a little exposure to the Glory can bring us the "peace that passes all understanding." Jesus said, "Come unto me and I will give you rest." He gives us rest in the Glory. Death cannot stand in the Glory. He raises the dead in the Glory. When we were still sinners living in our old nature, then our bodies may not be able to be in the glory. On the other hand, when the Lord calls the sinner, if the sinner responds properly to the Lords call, the glory will then bring life to the sinner as it did to me on the mountain side when I was 18 years old. My body was dead because of sin, but made alive because of the Fathers promise to send His Holy Spirit into me and quicken (make alive in the glory) my mortal body.

Romans 8:10-11

"And if Christ *be* in you, the body *is* dead because of sin; but the Spirit *is* life because of righteousness (innocence). But if the Spirit of him that raised up Jesus from the dead dwell in you, he that raised up Christ from the dead shall also quicken your mortal bodies by his Spirit that dwelleth in you."

Romans 6:13

"Neither yield ye your members *as* instruments of unrighteousness unto sin: but yield yourselves unto God, as those that are alive from the dead, and your members *as* instruments of righteousness unto God."

Jesus said:

John 5:25

"Verily, verily, I say unto you, The hour is coming, and now is, when the dead shall hear the voice of the Son of God: and they that hear shall live."

John 11:25

"Jesus said unto her, I am the resurrection, and the life: he that believeth in me, though he were dead, yet shall he live."

John 11:40

"Jesus saith unto her, Said I not unto thee, that, if thou wouldest believe, thou shouldest see the glory of God?" And then He raised Lazarus from the dead by the Glory of God.

The apostle Paul gave a list of those who had seen Jesus after His resurrection and then he includes himself in that list.

1Corinthians 15:3
"For I delivered unto you first of all that which I also received, how that Christ died for our sins according to the scriptures; And that he was buried, and that he rose again the third day according to the scriptures: And that he was seen of Cephas, then of the twelve: After that, he was seen of above five hundred brethren at once; of whom the greater part remain unto this present, but some are fallen asleep. After that, he was seen of James; then of all the apostles. And last of all he was seen of me also, as of one born out of due time."

So we can know by Paul's testimony that Jesus appeared to people even after He ascended to Heaven. The first time Jesus appeared to Paul, he was the only one who could see Him. The others that were with Paul couldn't see Him. So we know that Jesus clearly has the ability to make Himself seen only to those He wants to see Him and in the measure of Glory that He wants them to see Him. Paul lost his vision when he saw Jesus, because at that time, Paul was seeing the Glory shine so brightly from Jesus face and the Lord covered his eyes with scales to protect them (See Acts 9:18). I want to point out the fact that Paul was still a sinner when Jesus appeared to him on the road to Damascus. His body had not been quickened together with Christ yet. Once we are quickened together with Christ, we become replete with His glory. (See Ephesians 3:19) We were created in the image of God which is something that Lucifer could not say. We were created in His likeness so that we could contain His fullness. We were created for His glory. (See Isaiah 43:6-8) We were created in His likeness so that from us He could qualify us to be the bride for His Son, our Bridegroom. He created us in His likeness so that we could be like Him, arrayed in glory, filled with His fullness (See Ephesians 3:19) and so that we could be on a level that is suitable for Him to have satisfying communication with, so that THROUGH US, and AMONGST US, He could find the happiness that He longs for. We may have been born in sin, but we were predestined to be at His side for eternity, in glory. He wants to plan with us. He wants to rule and reign with us. He wants us to manage His affairs with Him. He wants us to rule over nations with Him. He has created us and qualified us to be in His likeness so that He can enjoy sharing all that He has with is. If we were not created in His image, we would not be capable of that, ever. No wonder the devil is jealous of us.

We receive garments of salvation and a robe of righteousness just as Jesus Himself was clothed with them according to Isaiah 61:10. We have an ability to stand in the glory and have the glory live in us, but the non-believer is unqualified and will not have the ability to see the glory in its brightness and live. That's what the scripture means when it says, "No man hath seen God at any time. If we love one another, God dwelleth in us, and his love is perfected in us." (See 1John 4:12) It means that "no sinner has seen God at any time."

1John 4:12 has been misquoted by many believers causing dismay and disbelief among many members in the Body of Christ. I experienced opposition to this by some ministers in China when I was there. One of them even tried to argue with me saying that Jesus wasn't raised from the dead with a physical body but rather only in spirit. When the apostle John was saying that "no many hath seen God at any time," he was making reference to those who have not experienced the regeneration experience of being quickened together with Christ in the heavenly places.

When you read the word "man" in the Greek, you discover that it means: "unworthy" or "unqualified" person. If we claim that no person who has been Born Again has or can see Jesus in His physical flesh and bones, then we deny His resurrection completely, because He appeared to many people AFTER His resurrection for extended periods of time. He was with His disciples for 40 days after His resurrection and had already been to heaven and back again. When He was first seen of Mary, He told her not to touch Him yet because He had not yet been to the Father. Then a few days later He tells Thomas to touch Him and see that He is flesh and bone. (See John 20:26-28) He also asked them to give Him fish and honeycomb to eat as evidence to the fact that He was flesh and bone. He was in His resurrected flesh and bone body. He didn't say He was flesh and blood, because the His glory was now the life of His flesh and bone, just as it will be in our resurrected bodies. "Behold my hands and my feet, that it is I myself: handle me, and see; for a spirit hath not flesh and bones, as ye see me have." (See Luke 24:37-43)

Between the time that Mary saw Him and when He saw the disciples, He had already been to Heaven with the Father to present His defense for the salvation of the world. That's where He presented His blood sacrifice and placed it on the mercy seat in Heaven in the True Tabernacle and now the Father can see us through the blood of Christ with eyes of mercy. He approached the Heavenly Father as the Great High Priest who was making intercession for all humanity.

When He appeared to His disciples in the house, the door was locked. He didn't knock on the door. He walked through the wall or was just translated there. (Luke 24:36) By walking about with His glorified flesh and bone body, He was showing us that flesh and bone can contain and maintain the glory of God. One day we too will be given NEW glorified bodies that are made of flesh and bone. The glory will be the life flow of it. We won't need blood in our veins any more. For now, we have been glorified with His glory in us (See Romans 8:17-19) and creation itself is waiting to experience this manifestation of it so that it too can be blessed by that glory in us too. (See Romans 8:20) Our bodies have been quickened by the Holy Spirit (See Romans 8:11) and for the most part we can live in physical health most of the time, yet we also are waiting to "And not only *they*, but ourselves also, which have the first fruits of the Spirit, even we ourselves groan within ourselves, waiting for the adoption, *to wit*, the redemption of our body." (Romans 8:23) Now we have a deposit, but later we will have the full redemption of our body. **2Co 1:22** Who hath also sealed us, and given the earnest of the Spirit (Gr.: "given in advance as a security deposit for the rest") in our hearts.

Romans 8:14
"For as many as are led by the Spirit of God, they are the sons of God."

Just as Jesus said, "Ye shall know them by their fruits." (See Matthew 7:16) It's the works of Jesus in our lives that reveal the glory of God to those around us. That's the fruits that Jesus was talking about. In Matthew 7, Jesus was referring to wolves in sheep's clothing. They appear good by "good works" in serving others, but have no signs and wonders following them. Those are the works Jesus talked about. John 14:12, Jesus said, "The works that I do also shall you do." What works did He do? Signs and wonders. Setting the captives free. Healing the sick, casting out devils, raising the dead. The wolves cannot produce those kind of works. That's how we can know the difference. For as many as are led by the Spirit of God, PROVE that they are the sons of God. This is the manifestation that the earth is groaning for. It's groaning for the manifestation of the glory that's in us NOW. If the devil can keep us from knowing that we are full of the glory, it can keep us down and make his work easier.

John 14:19
"Yet a little while, and the world seeth me no more; but ye see me: because I live, ye shall live also."

3John 1:11
"Beloved, follow not that which is evil, but that which is good. He that doeth good is of God: but he that doeth evil hath not seen God."

Ephesians 2:1
"And you *hath he quickened,* who were dead in trespasses and sins."

Ephesians 2:5
"Even when we were dead in sins, hath quickened us together with Christ, (by grace ye are saved;)"

Colossians 2:13
"And you, being dead in your sins and the uncircumcision of your flesh, hath he quickened together with him, having forgiven you all trespasses."

When the Lord appears to us in a dream or vision, it seems as real as if He was appearing to us in the flesh. It's only when the dream or vision is finished that we realize that it wasn't in the flesh. We then realize that it was a dream or vision.

1Kings 3:5
"In Gibeon the LORD appeared to Solomon in a dream by night: and God said, Ask what I shall give thee."

Matthew 1:20
"But while he thought on these things, behold, the angel of the Lord appeared unto him in a dream, saying, Joseph, thou son of David, fear not to take unto thee Mary thy wife: for that which is conceived in her is of the Holy Ghost."

Once He allows us to see His Glory in a high degree, the power of it takes over our flesh and we can no longer stand. He is the one who judges to what measure we are exposed to it. We could be on a stage with 50 other people when He exposes us to it in a measure that causes us to fall under the power of it and the others around us may feel nothing at all, just as it happened to the apostle Paul when he was on the road to Damascus and Jesus appeared to him with the bright shining Glory and he fell to the ground under the power of it, yet "the men which journeyed with him stood speechless, hearing a voice, but seeing no man." (See Acts 9:7)

For me personally, I mostly have seen Jesus in a vision or dream. When I see Him this way, it's very easy and comfortable for me to talk with Him. I feel "joy unspeakable and full of glory." (See 1Peter 1:8)

He Appeared At The Foot Of My Bed With His Glory:

One time I was fully conscious physically when He was standing at the foot of my bed. I woke up to the sound of my alarm, and when I was getting up out of my bed to reach it to turn it off, I saw Him there. I froze with my arm stretched out and my hand on the alarm. The alarm was set for the radio to turn on when it went off in the morning. I had set the radio to a Christian radio station and it was now playing praise and worship music.

At that moment, I didn't know how to respond! I was speechless! He was there, in a long white elegant robe. His face wasn't shining with light as I was expecting to see, and I wasn't overwhelmed with any fear of dying by the power of His Glory. In my mind I was saying to myself, "Say something to Him! Say something quickly before He disappears!" I then spoke out the first thing that came to my mind: "Lord, they're singing about You on the radio."

I felt so stupid for "stating the obvious!" But His response gave me an even bigger surprise! A big smile came on His face and suddenly light began to shine from His beautiful face. (I'm feeling goosebumps all over my body as I am writing this and the hair on my arms is standing up on end! Whenever I think or talk about that day, I have a smile come on my face and I don't even realize it. It seems that Christ in me, the hope of glory is smiling and it's His expression is on my face. Many times people have asked me, "Why are you smiling?" and I would say, "Oh, I didn't realize I was smiling!" A co-worker just asked me that a last week, saying, "Why do you smile so much?"

After the light of His Glory became visible to my eyes, something else became visible to my sight! Hold onto your seats, because it's spectacular and truly glorious!

The light that was shining from His face was moving in slow motion straight towards me. Light was not the only thing I observed coming from His face. Oh I wish that you will get a touch from Him regarding His glory as you read this! Out of His face was also coming small shinning clouds and huge droplets of water about the size of a softball! All in slow motion! The slow motion allowed me the time needed to observe it in detail. Some of the water droplets were elongated like a clown balloon and they were full of brilliant glowing light. The small clouds appeared soft and in all kinds rounded of shapes.

The light didn't travel in a straight line nor was it moving like a wave. It was flowing more like a ballerina, alive and a part of Himself.

The glory was travelling so elegantly towards me. I was still in a frozen position with my arm stretched out and my hand on the radio.

I was totally conscience of the fact that His glory was about to impact me, and when it did, the ecstatic feelings I was already experiencing escaladed! And suddenly out of my mouth came the most revelatory words: "This is the Love of God!" I had just had a head on collision with the Love of God, in slow motion! And suddenly I went backwards and it felt like I fell into the softest and most welcoming cloud. The light became so brilliant that all I could see now was light. My face was now smiling from ear to ear and I was feeling the greatest ecstasy I had ever experienced in my life before that time and until today.

I'm pausing from writing right now and leaning back in my chair, feeling the glory of God rising up in me and suddenly I heard the next song on my music player come on about seeing His face: "I wanna see Your Face and I wanna know Your Grace, O Lord." Those are the words that I'm listening to right now. It's no coincidence. He is speaking through the music, not only to me, but to all those reading this right now.

His Glory is so thick around me right now, that as I am breathing, the air I'm breathing in is very warm, as though I have my face in front of an open oven and am inhaling the heat pillowing out of it. This is how it happens for me when I am preaching. As I preach about His Glory, He begins manifesting Himself in our midst and everyone begins feeling it, not just me. There were many times in China when the air in the room was so thick with the glory of God, that I would stop preaching and invite everyone to come stand in a circle with me at the front of the church and lift our hands to Him and worship Him. At that time, people would be getting healed, delivered, and sometimes fall to the ground. Some would weep, some would laugh for joy of His Love colliding with them. Some would prophesy.

After I had this collision with the Love of God, I realized what happens in some churches, Believers conferences, Bible Studies in homes and the like. When we are gathered together in His name, He manifests Himself in His Glory. Like a ballerina, He dances around us, touching each and every one of us as we praise and worship Him. His Love collides with us and He connects with us in the deepest way. God is Love! God is a spirit! God is light! That's who and what He is in our midst and in our hearts and as we gather together in His name. He comes and dwells in our midst in all His fullness.

After we have been with Him this way, our hearts are enlarged and we are changed from glory to glory by the Spirit of the Lord. (See 2Corinthians 3:18) We stand in His midst with unveiled faces, beholding the glory. This is what changes us into His image. It's His glory that changes us. We all know how much we change when we fall in love with the person that we will marry. We suddenly become so soft hearted and exceptionally attentive to doing anything to please them. So it is with us when we collide with the Love of God. We become more like Him and people know us by our love because now we love exceptionally more than we did before. It doesn't mean that we are the most loving person on the planet, but it does mean that in one degree or another, our hearts have enlarged and we are more loving than we were before. This is what people see in us. They see how much we've changed. That's the contrast that makes the difference to people's opinions of us.

I remember one of my ministry students in China. She was a new believer when I met her. Prior to her meeting Jesus, her life was like an American Country Song. Her family left her. Her husband left her. She was depressed and feeling suicidal, until one day, she observed two foreigners sitting on a bench near the entrance to a mall. Her attention was drawn to them because she saw how happy they looked as they were both reading from the same book at the same time. She thought that was odd and out of curiosity she approached them and asked them what they were reading. They hesitantly told her that they were reading the Bible. The young girl asked them what it was about. The foreigners, being surprised by such a question, said, "It's about Jesus of course. Have you never heard of Him?" She said, "No. Who is He? Can you tell me about Him?"

I will call this girl Lucy. Lucy attentively listened to them as they shared with her about Jesus. They then asked her if she would like to accept Him as her Lord and Savior. She accepted the invitation and said a prayer for salvation with them. Six months later, one of those foreigners, whom I had just recently met, invited Lucy to one of my House Miracle meetings and told Lucy to bring as many friends as possible. She brought about four others with her. Three of the four she brought with her accepted Jesus as their Lord and Savior in that meeting that day.

I then had the chance to invite Lucy to keep coming to the ministry training meetings and soon she opened up her house for me to hold one ministry training there each week. In several months, I witnessed the Lord's Love through Lucy first touch her husband and then the rest of her family. Her husband moved home and soon accepted Jesus as his Lord and Savior. Her mother moved back in with her and soon accepted Jesus as her Lord and Savior and both her mother and husband began coming to ministry training and miracle meetings. Then Lucy began going to her home town and evangelizing her whole family. Uncles, aunts, cousins, and friends were accepting Jesus as their Lord and Savior. Every day Lucy took the taxi to her new restaurant where she and two foreigners were reaching out to the public and leading hundreds to Jesus for salvation. Every time she was in a taxi, she would lead the driver to accept Jesus as Lord and Savior. When she was shopping in the markets for food for the restaurant, she was often was lead to talk about Jesus to others and then lead them in a prayer for salvation right there in the market place.

I could say a lot more testimonies for Lucy, but I want to share now with you about the power that Lucy had in her testimony. She was the most meek person I think I ever met. Her life was destitute and Jesus came in a picked up all the pieces with His Love. She was suicidal. But Loved picked her up and gave her a sense of belonging. Wherever she went, she wanted to tell people what Jesus did for her. She would tell people like this: "Can I share something with you? You won't believe how low my life had become. My husband left me because I was so mean to him. My mother left my home because she couldn't handle how controlling I was over her. My uncles and aunts, brother and cousins thought I was the worst person in the world. I wanted to end my life. I felt so alone. Then one day I saw these two foreigners reading this book together so I went and asked them what it was. It seemed I was intruding on them, but I was so curious to know why they looked so happy. When I asked them about what they were reading, they told me that the book is about Jesus but I didn't know who Jesus was and they explained Him to me. They explained that He would change my life for the good. I believed them and said a prayer to accept Him as my Lord and Savior. Since that time, I have felt so loved by Jesus that my husband and family took notice to the change in my attitude. My husband asked me why I was so different. When I told him that it was because of Jesus, he said that if Jesus was so powerful to change me like that, he also wanted Jesus and he moved back home with me and we bought a house together.

I apologized to my mother and all my family and they watched the change in me and wanted to know what changed me. When I told them it was Jesus, they were so amazed by the great change and wanted Him too."

After Lucy shared this with people, their hearts were softened by the Love of God that was flowing from Lucy's testimony and would accept the invitation to say a prayer for salvation. One time a taxi driver said to Lucy, would you come with me to my home and share this with my wife too? If she hears your story, maybe she will accept Jesus and become more loving to me."

There were several times when I would walk into Lucy's restaurant, and she would say to me: "Brother, so good to see you! Please come meet my new friends! They all just accepted Jesus as their Lord and Savior! I told them about you. Would you please come and tell them about the Holy Spirit and pray for them to receive Him!" I would then sit down and share with that family or group of friends about the Holy Spirit and Lucy would translate for me. This happened many times.

Lucy's heart was won over by the Love of God and in the time that I knew her, I heard of probably over a thousand people accepting Jesus as Lord and Savior through her testimony. That was in about 7 months.

Each one of us are touched in a different measure. We can't compare our encounter with the Lord to others. Each one of us are different, but we do have one thing in common: Once we have collided with the Love of God, we change for the good. I never had the same effect in sharing my testimony with others like Lucy had and I never meant anyone else who had the same effect when sharing their testimony since that time or before that. Lucy's testimony is a powerful one and we can personally grow from it. In fact, the Lord has used her testimony to influence change in my personal life. I'm very thankful for that.

To me, Lucy was chosen by the Lord in a similar way that He chose to use the Samaritan woman at the well. She had been previously married five times. She must have had a lot of hard times that broke her and others hearts. She may have even been in the midst of major turmoil in her life at that time when Jesus met her. She may have been experiencing suicidal thoughts like Lucy had been. Jesus then revealed to her that He was the Messiah and she ran and told people throughout the city and they came to Jesus seeking to speak with Him. They then proclaimed that they now believe on Jesus, not just because of the woman's testimony, but because of things He told them.

John 4:28-30
"The woman then left her waterpot, and went her way into the city, and saith to the men, Come, see a man, which told me all things that ever I did: is not this the Christ? Then they went out of the city, and came unto him."

The coming of the Kingdom of God is the heavenly places coming on earth as they are in Heaven and Jesus removed the veil from three of His disciples eyes to see it. Consider everything they saw: Jesus was transfigured before them. His raiment became shining. They were seeing the Kingdom of God with Power. **The clothing that was upon Jesus and the cloud that overshadowed them was the Power of the Kingdom of God at hand.** I have seen this with my very eyes many times because He allowed me to see it. This is what Jesus was revealing to them and it was written for all nations, so that they might believe that Jesus is the Christ, the Son of God:

John 20:30-31

"And many other signs truly did Jesus in the presence of his disciples, which are not written in this book: But these are written, that ye might believe that Jesus is the Christ, the Son of God; and that believing ye might have life through his name."

It's our very presence on this earth that's keeping the devil from doing what He really wished He could do. We are hosting the Kingdom of God within us and the glory of God is radiating from us just as they saw it radiating from Jesus. We are His flesh on earth, and as His flesh, we are hosting His glory and His Power.

He told them that they would see the Kingdom of God COME with POWER. Did it come? It came and it's here now. Was it the first time it had come? No. It had come upon Jesus when He was baptized in the Jordan by John the Baptist. John saw the Heaven open and the Spirit of God descend upon Him and it remained upon Him. (See John 1:32)

Using My Imagination To Trigger My Spiritual Senses:

I spent about 8 months working just part time before my trip to China. The five or so days that I wasn't working, I would spend most of my time at home, sitting in the Presence of the Lord. I would have my Bible at hand and my praise and worship music playing in the background. I would close my eyes most of the time and just wait on Him. I would feel His Presence intensify throughout my time with Him. It was such a wonderful time with Him.

Since I returned from China, I am able to enter into His glory on a higher level. I understand His glory more now than I did before. I know what's happening around me in the heavenly places more than I did then, and because of that, I am able to enter into a deeper experience with Him more often and more easily.

We are changed from glory to glory. So we can know that as we are walking in the glory, we will be changed into His image more and more each day. (See 2Corinthians 3:18)

When I sit waiting on Him, I imagine the robe upon me. I imagine the wind of the Holy Ghost blowing under it. I imagine that Jesus is with me and in me in the heavenly places. (See Ephesians 2:4) While that's happening, I begin feeling that heavenly atmosphere become tangible around me. Joy begins to fill me up and I feel the glory shining from my face. Suddenly I am smiling and I didn't even realize it. I imagine that His Light is glowing from the robe. I imagine that His glory cloud is all around me.

Standing In The Glory:

When I met my friend who has the baptism of fire, he invited me to attend a house meeting at his home. It was winter time, and I remember wondering why the heater was on so high. I asked him, and he told me that it had been off all day. The heat was the baptism of fire that was tangible in the atmosphere. It was so hot that I couldn't even keep my socks on!

At his house meeting, he would put some soft praise and worship music on quietly in the background and we would stand or sit in the room with hands uplifted or in a receiving position at our sides near our waist. The fire was radiating throughout the room, and just as radiation is contagious, so was the fire. When I left that place, I was walking in it in my ministry and have been ever since.

Today, in my prayer times, I often will stand and wait on the Lord just as when in his house. The fire comes, the wind comes, the clouds come, the river comes, because the Lord is here and I am standing in the heavenly places on earth. I normally begin in the standing position, then when I feel led, I will get on my knees until I'm finished. His Love pours out mightily. It's very intimate. Truly, those who are joined to the Lord are one spirit with Him.

1Corinthians 6:15-17

"Know ye not that your bodies are the members of Christ? shall I then take the members of Christ, and make *them* the members of an harlot? God forbid. What? know ye not that he which is joined to an harlot is one body? for two, saith he, shall be one flesh. But he that is joined unto the Lord is one spirit."

His Glory Cloud Became Visible To The Entire Church:

Sometimes the cloud of His Presence was visible for the entire church to witness. I am not the only one who saw it. Dozens of witnesses saw it. The miracles that took place were so incredible. The people's lives were so changed by the glory. Sometimes people would come and explain in detail how they saw Jesus' robe flowing past them in the isle as they were listening to my message. The people wanted to know more about it and asked the pastor to keep me after the meeting so they could do a questions and answers time. I sat with about 13 of the leaders in a big circle and they asked me what was on their minds about what happened. I explained it to them as best as I could. Today I understand it much better than even at that time.

The important thing is that as many people as possible learn from this and begin to see it happen in their own lives and ministry and take it to the ends of the earth, or even just to their own household. Some of us are called to nations, while others of us are called to reach our household. It's important to realize that we are not all called to the same calling.

I Saw Thousands Of Angels Worshipping The Lord:

One time I was laying on my bed in the middle of the day to have a time of praise and worship. I wasn't tired at all. I often had times when I wanted to praise the Lord laying down. I enjoy it. This one day, when I lay on my bed with hands raised up, I suddenly heard footsteps in my house on the floor below. I knew there was nobody else in the house besides me, so at first I was a little worried. Nonetheless, I kept praising the Lord, only I was now singing more quietly.

I heard the footsteps coming up the stairs towards my bedroom. They were moving slowly. I wanted to call out for who it was, but I didn't. I just kept praising the Lord. My bedroom door was open and I heard the footsteps approaching it. To my surprise, once the footsteps reached my door, there was nobody there physically, but I knew there was someone there. I kept praising the Lord with hands uplifted. I then heard the footsteps walk into my room right to my bedside and stop, when suddenly, the edge of my bed sunk down a little and I could see the imprint of someone sitting on it. I kept praising the Lord. I didn't feel fearful at all. I felt safe and I was feeling the peace that passes all understanding. I knew that it must be the Angel of the Lord.

Suddenly, my room disappeared and all I could now see around me was the stars and planets in our solar system. But I was not alone. All around me suddenly appeared a multitude of angels and they were praising the Lord with loud voices. I felt the heightened ecstasy beyond imagination. We were in clouds and the Light of His glory was so brilliant. I began to join with the angles in praise. It seemed to last for a long time before I was back in my room just as before.

It would take me weeks to share all the stories of the similar testimonies. I have seen angels dancing in the church while leading in worship. I have seen the Lord face to face in visions and dreams more times than I can even imagine. The Lord is no respector of persons. These are the things that happen when He pours out His Spirit upon all flesh. Visions, dreams and prophecies are all a part of the Pentecostal outpouring that the Lord Jesus asked the Heavenly Father to send on earth in fulfilment of His Promise to Abraham and all that have faith in Him with our Father Abraham.

Galatians 3:13-14
"Christ hath redeemed us from the curse of the law, being made a curse for us: for it is written, Cursed *is* every one that hangeth on a tree: That the blessing of Abraham might come on the Gentiles through Jesus Christ; that we might receive the promise of the Spirit through faith." (See also Acts 1:4; Luke 24:49; Acts 2:33)

When the day of Pentecost came, it could be heard and seen. There was the sound of the wind from Heaven and tongues of fire upon the heads of the Believers. This was a fulfilment of what the Father promised to do. Since that time, these same signs and wonders still occur in small pockets around the world. Besides happening to me, I know others personally who experience it. I have one friend who told me last year that when he was preaching in Taiwan, his voice couldn't be heard over the microphone because the sound of the wind from Heaven was too loud. His testimonies are credible, for I have done a little travelling and ministry with him. The Lord mentored me through this man's ministry in part. I have seen things that I can't write about. Jesus said to be careful where we cast our pearls. There's so much more happening around the world by the Holy Ghost that most Believers have never even imagined could be possible.

More verses about Righteousness:

Romans 5:17-21

"For if by one man's offence death reigned by one; much more they which receive abundance of grace and of **the gift of righteousness (Gr. Innocence)** shall reign in life by one, Jesus Christ. Therefore as by the offence of one *judgment came* upon all men to condemnation; even so by the righteousness of one *the free gift came* upon all men **unto justification (Gr. Innocence) of life.** For as by one man's disobedience many were made sinners, so by the obedience of one **shall many be made righteous (Gr. Innocent).** Moreover the law entered, that the offence might abound. But where sin abounded, grace did much more abound: That as sin hath reigned unto death, **even so might grace reign through (innocence) righteousness** unto eternal life by Jesus Christ our Lord."

Romans 10:4

"For Christ *is* the end of the law for righteousness (innocence) to every one that believeth."

Galatians 2:21

"I do not frustrate the grace of God: for **if righteousness (innocence) *come* by the law, then Christ is dead in vain.**"

1Corinthians 1:30

"But of him are ye in Christ Jesus, who of God **is made unto us wisdom, and righteousness (innocence),** and sanctification, and redemption."

Philippians 3:9

"And be found in him, **not having mine own righteousness (innocence),** which is of the law, but that which is through the faith of Christ, **the righteousness (innocence) which is of God by faith.**"

Beijing Bell Tower. Originally built as a musical instrument, at the time of the Han Dynasty (206 BC-220), there was 'a morning bell and a dusk drum'.

Bells From the Tomb of Marquis Yi of Zeng, dated 433 BC. These are displayed the Hubei Provincial Museum where I visited frequently. Entry is free to encourage historical remembrance.

Chongqing Arhat Temple is one of the most famous Buddhist Temples in China. It is located in Yuzhong District, and is now the seat of the Chongqing Buddhism Association.

East Lake City Park. I rode my bicycle through it most weekends. It has many man-made landscapes rich in culture from the Chu Dynasty.

East Lake in Wuhan. It has a twisty shoreline of 112 km. It took me half the day to ride my bike around just a small portion of it. I did that most weekends for exercise and sightseeing.

Electric and Gas powered Bikes very popular in China. There are bike parking areas like this everywhere. You pay an attendant to watch your bike while you shop or work.

Former Wuhan Univ. Library. It's now too old and unsafe to be used as a library. It's only a 10 minute bike ride from my previous home.

Hiking up the highest mountain in Chongqing. The cloud cover is moisture, not smog. I became friends with a policeman there and we would go on day hikes in different parts of the city.

I was trying on some traditional Chinese Clothing in Wuhan.

Inside the Grand Ocean Mall in Wuhan. This mall catered
mostly to students. Wuhan is the universtity capital of China.
There are approximately 1 million students in that city.

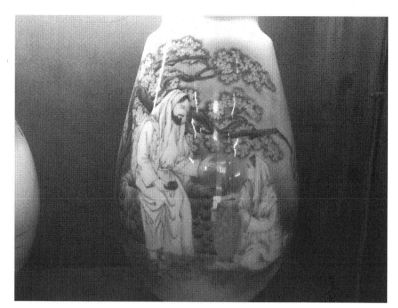

Jesus with Samaritan Woman at the well on this piece of custom made porcelain. I was friends with the Christian family who owned the store. They put scripture on the bottom of every piece.

11/19/2010

My Daily Food Bowl and chopsticks. This bowl and set of chopsticks were a gift from my friends Porcelain shop.

My faithful Bike! This Bicycle took me miles and miles around Wuhan. It was a very useful bike. There was a bike mechanic close to my home I became friends with. He always tuned it for me.

My team went back to continue my ministry in this village 2 weeks after I left, and the police were there waiting, hoping to arrest me for preaching, confirming my date of departure from China.

Old Missionaries house in Wuhan. Approximately 150 years old.

Signing my name and adding a Bible Verse in the
guest book at The Dream Cafe in Wuhan.

The 7 stories high Grand Ocean Mall in Wuhan where I shopped weekly.

The Road I lived on in Wuhan, directly beside Wuhan University.

These are Funeral Gifts for someone who died and lived in my building. This is outside my house door. The event, with loud speakers lasted for two days, night and day.

This is a former dorm for male students at Wuhan University.

This is a statue of the 1st president of China. January 1, 1912,
returning from the US, Sun Yat sen became the provisional
president of the new ROC (Republic of China).

Very old temple on the highest mountain in Chongqing.

Wuhan City from a tall building top. You can see the longest river in China runs right through the city.

Wuhan University. All students must spend their first year in military training.

Wuhan. I was out touring the city along the Yanzi River (Long River), which is what I normally did every Sunday.

HOLY SPIRIT BAPTISM

Chapter 6

Why was preaching about the Holy Spirit Baptism so important in China? It's because that even in the government churches it's against the law to preach about the Holy Spirit and the baptism. Imagine if it was against the law in our country? What if you could go to prison for preaching about Him? Imagine if we had government spies who pretended to be Christians attending our church services and reporting everything we did. This is the condition of the Christian churches in China. There are camera's all around the government churches and spies who attend the churches.

One church in particular that I had visited several times, was shut down in about 2005 for having too much of a membership growth. They were having great success in reaching the youth and the church multiplied in size quickly. It scared the government and they shut the church down for one year before allowing them to assume weekly services under supervision. By that time most of the sheep had already scattered and were no longer attending anywhere or were going elsewhere for fellowship. There are video cameras around the church building that have government staff members keeping track of how many people come into the parking lot and into the building each day. When there is too much change, red flags raise up and they respond accordingly. There's a Christian book store beside that church building. I went in there and was so surprised that they were not allowed to sell Bibles there and none of the Christian books were allowed to have the Bible in it except for some quotes. Only some Government churches are allowed to sell Bibles in the church and the government decides how many and which version.

In all the government supervised churches in China, the pastors have to get a degree through one of the government Bible schools. In those schools, the students will learn what they can and can't teach in the churches. They will be made to fear the consequences of disobeying.

In every city and village there is a government agency that employs agents to work as spies and investigate all the government churches and try to find out where the underground churches are located so that they can infiltrate them. It's very difficult to locate the underground churches in China. Some cities it's more difficult than others. In some cities there's less religious suppression than others. Take Tibet for example. When one of my translators was there on a mission trip, she sent a text message to her sister in mainland China and used the word Jesus in the text. She then left that house and heard from the others in the house that the police had come 10 minutes after she left looking for her to arrest her. On the other hand, if you're in a city such as Shenzhen, then there is a lot less pressure on what is preached. Nonetheless, even when they have less pressure, in most cases they don't even know how to preach about the Holy Spirit because they have not had the teaching about it.

So needless to say, whenever I preached the Holy Spirit Baptism in any city or village I was in, the response was almost always every person in the church coming forward to receive it. They never heard of such good news! They were so excited about it! I will share with you the scripture the Lord had me share with them to show them about their need of the Holy Spirit baptism.

Ephesians 3:20
"Now unto him that is able to do exceeding abundantly above all that we ask or think, according to the power that worketh in us."

The thing is that in China this is a very common scripture for the preachers to preach. This is what I was often told. The one difference between what they were hearing and what I was preaching, was that last part of verse 20: "according to the power that worketh in us." I asked them if they experience this scripture in their lives? They didn't put up their hands. I would then ask them if they would like to experience the Lord answering their prayers abundantly above all they could ask or think. They said a big "Amen!" I would ask them, "how many people here know what is the power that the apostle Paul is referring to here?" Nobody knew. Nobody ever had the answer for that question, until I told them. I told them that it's the power of the Holy Spirit that comes upon us when we are baptized with Him and fire. I would then ask how many of them ever were baptized with the Holy Spirit? And nobody ever lifted their hand up. Then I would ask them, "How many people here would like to receive the baptism of the Holy Spirit, which is the promise of your Heavenly Father?" Every hand would go up.

I would explain to them Acts 1:8. In Acts 1:8 Jesus was explaining that there would be power come upon them by the Holy Ghost. This would make them witnesses of Him and His resurrection. I told them that this was the power that Paul was talking about that comes upon us and in us. It's the promised Holy Spirit and by Him in us and upon us, God is able to do abundantly above all that we ask or think. Not just for us, but for our families, friends and coworkers. The Chinese are Big on family, so this meant a lot to them.

Before I even laid hands on them for the baptism, I would ask them, "How many of you are feeling fire on your heads? I mean, how many feel a strong heat moving over your heads?" Every hand would go up. The Holy Spirit was coming upon them before I even prayed for the baptism for them. It's just like Cornelius. Peter didn't have to lay hands for them to be baptized. He just shared the Good News of the Power of the Holy Spirit that came upon Jesus and when He did, the same power came upon them.

Acts 10:38, 44
"How God anointed Jesus of Nazareth with the Holy Ghost and with power: who went about doing good, and healing all that were oppressed of the devil; for God was with him. While Peter yet spoke these words, the Holy Ghost fell on all them which heard the word."

I don't know how many believers were baptized through my ministry there, but I'm sure it's over 1,000. It was only in the last two months that I was there that the Lord directed me to do so. Before that I didn't preach the baptism of the Holy Spirit everywhere I went. I preached that the Kingdom of Heaven was at hand and within each believer. I preached that Jesus is doing the same things today that He did 2,000 years ago because He's alive and He changes not.

In every meeting I ever preached in the last nine months that I was there, the wind and fire manifested. People felt the wind and the fire all over the room. It was the atmosphere of Heaven in our midst and in that atmosphere was the very power of the Holy Ghost performing miracles. He was setting the captives free.

In those last nine months, I was living in one city and training a team that grew to the size of 80 members before I left back to Canada. It was a small city of about fifteen million people. I had heard of a massive outpouring of the Holy Spirit in churches in China, but outside of China we have no idea where those churches are. We don't know what cities they are located in. Guess what? I never found any outpouring of the Holy Spirit in any of the churches or cities I went to. Either they are so hidden that I couldn't find them, or they were nonexistent in the cities I was in. At least all the church leaders I was working with never even heard that there was any kind of Holy Spirit outpouring anywhere in China. They were completely oblivious to the whole thing. This really amazed me. Every city and every village I went to, they never heard of such a thing, and I went to more cities and villages than I can count. Regardless of the fact that I found none of the so called revivals happening there, I was experiencing one wherever I went and the Lord was doing it through me and the believers I was training. I kept hoping to find a group of believers who knew about the crying saints who met in caves and who had all night prayer meetings often. I never met one.

This is to say, that, everywhere I was setting Holy Ghost fires, was a place that never even knew anything about it. So, what does that mean for the rest of the church around the world? If you want to experience the fire of the Holy Ghost, then go to China as an English teacher, or just as a short term missionary or become a student in one of their universities, and ask the Lord to lead you and your spouse to the right people who want you to help them in their churches. Tell them about the Holy Spirit and fire. When you do, the Lord will confirm that word with signs following because in China, there's a wave of prayers reaching up to Heaven and the Lord is responding to those prayers for the whole nation. Even in places that are not praying, the Lord is still responding to the prayers in the other provinces and other cities and villages.

China is being invaded by Heaven, make no mistake about that.

Being a missionary in China as I was is not for everyone. It's dangerous because it's against the law for foreigners to preach in China. Presently, in 2014, the Chinese government is increasing their investigations to find foreigners preaching in their country and shut them down. When we go there and start Holy Ghost fires, the government takes it very seriously, but that never stopped the apostles from preaching. They were threatened. They were beaten. They were commanded not to preach in the name of Jesus Christ, but that never stopped them. The Chinese people are crying out to God to help them because in some provinces they are being told to stop or they will be beaten, tortured and killed. It's this persecution that is pressuring them to call out to God just as the Jews who were enslaved to Egypt were calling out to God to save them. When the Jews cried out to be set free, the Lord came with a mighty hand and delivered them with signs and wonders. Heaven is invading China today in response to the cry of God's people, and make no mistake about it: He WILL set the captives free. "Let my people go!"

FAITH

Chapter 7

The God given kind of faith only comes from the Word of God. In order for that to happen, we need to have a revelation of His Word as given by His Holy Spirit. We need to rely upon Him to reveal His Word and thereby bring us the needed faith to activate the promises of God. Receiving revelation from the Holy Spirit also requires faith, so I want to begin this chapter by sharing with you some promises in the Word of God that will impart supernatural faith to receive revelation from the Holy Spirit concerning His Promises.

1Corinthians 2:9-10 "But as it is written, Eye hath not seen, nor ear heard, neither have entered into the heart of man, the things which God hath prepared for them that love him. But God hath revealed *them* unto us by his Spirit: for the Spirit searcheth all things, yea, the deep things of God."

The important part of the above two verses is that "God hath revealed them unto us by his Spirit." No evil eye or ear has heard the things which God hath prepared for them that love him.

1John 2:20
"But ye have an unction (from the Holy One, and ye know all things."

The word "unction" in the Greek reads like this: "*smearing*, that is, (figuratively) the special *endowment* ("chrism") of the Holy Spirit: - anointing, unction."

John 16:13

"Howbeit when he, the Spirit of truth, is come, he will guide you into all truth: for he shall not speak of himself; but whatsoever he shall hear, *that* shall he speak: and he will shew you things to come."

Ponder on these above verses for a few minutes and ask the Holy Ghost to reveal it to you. Once He reveals them to you, supernatural faith will become active for you in regards to those specific promises. Once we have faith for His Promise(s), we then ask for them with full confidence in the natural. Supernatural faith is supernatural and when we have that, our natural confidence will always follow. If we don't have supernatural faith that comes by revelation of the Word of God, then our natural confidence will be weak and a stumbling block to activating those Promises of God that we see in His Word.

Ponder on the following Promise of God as He inspired the apostle John to write:

1John 5:14-15

"And this is the confidence that we have in him, that, if we ask any thing according to his will (Word/Promise(s)), he heareth us: And if we know that he hear us, whatsoever we ask, we know that we have the petitions that we desired of him."

His Word is His will in writing, just as we receive a receipt when we buy an item in a store. It's His Guarantee. The receipt cannot be denied by the company. It's a "Proof Of Purchase." God's Words are His Promises to humanity and can be used as receipts of His Will to us. His Words are His Bond. They cannot be denied when we ask in the name of His Son Jesus Christ. So in other words, if we can find a promise of God for a thing, we simply ask for a revelation of that Promise so that we can receive supernatural faith to act upon. Once we have the supernatural faith, and put action to our faith, we activate that promise of God and we even will have natural confidence to see it come to pass. We will feel the joy of the Lord and glory of God fill us. We simply keep giving thanks for it until it comes to pass. Sometimes our faith reaps the fulfillment of a promise instantly, in seconds, minutes, hours, days or at times weeks. In the oddest occasions it may take years for something such as our faith to purchase a new house, or buy a new car.

We activate the promises of God in our lives through the action of faith. For example: The Bible says that we enter His presence with singing. (Psalm 100:1) So if we want to enter His Presence, we activate that promise of God by the action of faith by singing praises to His name, majesty and glory and we begin to worship and adore Him. Through that action, by faith in the fact of the Promises of God, that they are true Promises and cannot lie, we are now activating those Promises to come to pass in our lives. At the same time, we are fulfilling His command to seek first His kingdom and His righteousness (innocence). The outcome of our seeking, is that, all things will be added unto us. (See Matthew 6:33) That's one of His Promises.

The action of faith is the visible substance of invisible faith:

Mark 2:4-5
"And when they could not come nigh unto him for the press, they uncovered the roof where he was: and when they had broken *it* up, they let down the bed wherein the sick of the palsy lay. When Jesus saw their faith, he said unto the sick of the palsy, Son, thy sins be forgiven thee."

The two friends couldn't get in the door where Jesus was because the place was packed full of people, so they came through the roof to reach Him. Their action of coming through the roof was the visible proof of their invisible faith. They had heard the promises of God and received a revelation from the Holy Spirit regarding them. They were so excited to see Jesus heal their friend that they couldn't wait for Jesus to come out of the house where He was preaching. Their faith was so powerful that they just came through the roof. Nothing was going to stop them from receiving the Promise of God for healing.

There was a woman who was like that in China. She heard of the miracles that Jesus was doing in my meetings and would walk up five floors of stairs to come once a week for five weeks. One leg was about 12 inches shorter than the other. She had to pull herself up those stairs using the railing, but she had received a revelation from the Holy Ghost about the Promise of God to heal her if she will keep coming to Him by faith. I pointed her out each week while preaching and said: "This woman's leg is going to grow out one of these weeks if she will keep coming to Jesus by her faith in Him. You will see it because she is putting action to her supernatural faith for a miracle and Jesus honors that kind of faith." After five weeks, while I was preaching, the Lord spoke to me saying, "This is her day. Today she will walk."

I stopped preaching and went over in front of her where she was sitting in the front row, and said to her: "This is your day. Today you will walk." Then I continued preaching. I had received the Word of God that today was her day and that I wasn't to pray for her until I finished preaching. After I finished preaching, I invited her to the front of the church where I was preaching and asked her to sit on a chair. I crouched down in front of her and picked up both feet and said, "In the name of Jesus Christ of Nazareth I command this leg to grow out to normal!"

My translator was beside me. As soon as I said those words, the leg that was 12 inches shorter from birth grew out in about one second flat! My translator and I looked at each other and said, "Praise the Lord!" I then said to the woman, "Stand up and walk!" She stood up and started walking totally normally for the first time since she was born! Thank You Jesus! The church started yelling praises to the Lord! This woman continued to come to meetings until I left China. I have her picture in group pictures that I took while I was there.

Now that I have supernatural faith from the Holy Spirit concerning miracles, I have complete natural confidence that the Lord WILL confirm His Words with signs following. I preach confidently. I tell the people they WILL be healed once they have the supernatural faith in His Word which is His Guarantee to do a thing.

When we purchase a new car, it comes with a warranty, or call it a guarantee. If the car stops working before the warranty is expired, then we return it to the car dealership where we bought it, show them our receipt and they are obligated to fulfill their warranty by repairing it. God's Promises are the same. God cannot lie. If He promises to do a thing, He is obligated to fulfill it. This is what I see in His Word and this is how I preach. It's supernatural faith for me as given by the Holy Spirit who guided me into all truth and revealed this to me.

The warranty on our new cars have an expiry date and once that expiry date has come, then the car dealership is no longer required to repair any problems with our car at no charge to us. The Word of God is not like that. It has no expiry date.

Numbers 11:23
"And the LORD said unto Moses, Is the LORD'S hand waxed short? thou shalt see now whether my word shall come to pass unto thee or not." Jesus is the LORD'S hand and His hand is not waxed short. As we gather together in His name, He is walking in the midst of us. (See Acts 11:21 "And the hand of the Lord was with them: and a great number believed, and turned to unto the Lord.")

1Peter 1:24-25
"For all flesh *is* as grass, and all the glory of man as the flower of grass. The grass withereth, and the flower thereof falleth away: But the word of the Lord endureth for ever. And this is the word which by the gospel is preached unto you."

I stood in front of crowds as small as 12 people and as large as 700 and told them that "Jesus is alive and Anointed with the Holy Ghost and Power, and He guaranteed us that where two or three are gathered in His name He WILL be there. Therefore He IS here today and guarantees to give a witness of His resurrection with Signs following. (See Mark 16:20) He WILL heal in response to God Given faith as inspired by His Promises to heal you. So I will share with you His Promises and He will reveal them to you. Once He does, you will receive supernatural faith. Once you put action to that faith, He guarantees to heal you. If He is dead, then nothing will happen. If He's alive, ... and He is ... then He WILL do the same things today that He did 2,000 years ago. He WILL heal you. If nothing happens today, then you can call me a liar and kick me out. But if and when you see Jesus guarantee His Word as

I present it to you today, then you can act on your faith and praise the Lord for healing you."

The Lord always confirmed His Word as I presented it to the people this way. Miracles always happened. There was never a time that miracles didn't happen. His name was always glorified. Jesus IS alive and IS still doing the same things today that He did 2,000 years ago. He hasn't changed, as some today claim He has. He's still casting out devils, healing the sick and diseased, and raising the dead.

There were people coming to my weekly miracle meetings from all over China. I didn't get to know many of them because of the language barrier but there was one woman who I recognized that had been driving from her city three hours away every Tuesday to experience the Presence of the Holy Ghost Fire and see Jesus healing people.

For months I didn't know she was traveling so far. Then one week she brought her son because it happened to be a government holiday for the schools. He was totally blind in his left eye. I laid my hand over his eye and commanded the spirit of blindness to leave him in Jesus name. Then someone held up one of his school papers while he covered his good eye. I asked him to read the paper from about 3 feet away and he began reading clearly with the eye that was blind. Thank You Jesus! The mother was so excited and so was the boy.

About 2 weeks later she brought with her 7 church leaders from her church. I didn't know they knew each other until after the meeting when she introduced them to me and asked me if I would bless them.

They lined up and I prayed for them one by one. Then the last one, who was woman, had her head and shoulders bowed forward because she was under great physical distress due to several diseases in her body. I prayed a blessing for her and I heard the Lord tell me that He was healing her.

I asked her how she was feeling and she told me that she felt no difference. I said to her, that's OK, because Jesus told me that He's healing you and you're are going to feel better soon." She said amen and they stayed awhile and talked with us before they left.

Before we even left the church building, they called my translator, saying, "She's healed! She's healed just like Jesus said! Ask if the brother will come with his team to preach in our churches." They were driving down the highway on their way home and suddenly the power of the Lord came upon her and totally healed her! When I saw her a couple of weeks later, she came to me with the others and was shouting and waving her arms in the air and showing me how she can move freely now. She was ecstatic and praising the Lord with her arms uplifted towards Heaven.

Well, we went there two weeks later. We rented a bus as we always did when going to preach in other cities or villages and sixteen members from my ministry team of 80 were with me. We sang praises most of the way there.

One week prior to us going there, the Lord told my translator in a dream to pray all week for the Lord to show us what He wanted to do in this city when we went there. He then told her that there would be hundreds of people. He told me that there would be many deaf and blind people and to pray for them all at the same time.

When we arrived at the church building we were amazed at the size of it. It was huge!

That night I had a dream that I was placed in prison in China. When I was in prison I remembered talking to different people in there and I told them that I wouldn't be in there long. One fella in the prison told me that I would never get out because NOBODY ever gets out. I then told him that they couldn't hold me because I had done nothing wrong.

I then woke from the dream and the Lord immediately downloaded the message I was to preach on the two churches we were going to that day. It was basically this: "Death could not hold Jesus in the grave because He had no sin and death cannot hold YOU because you now stand before God as if you never sinned! You are justified. Your sins have been accounted for by the blood of the Lamb of God. JUST-AS-IF-YOU-NEVER-SINNED! He took the fall for YOU! Death has to let you go! I cannot hold you! It has no legal right anymore, for you are not justified by the works of the law, but by faith in Jesus Christ so that you can be saved by the grace of God without being held accountable for your sins. Jesus accounted for your sins. "Bless the LORD, O my soul, and forget not all his benefits: Who forgiveth all thine iniquities; who healeth all thy diseases; Who redeemeth thy life from destruction; who crowneth thee with loving, kindness and tender mercies;" (See Psalm 103:2-4)

The gospel was preached in fullness. I asked the whole church to hold their hand in front of them. I then asked them how far away is your hand from yourself? That's how far away the Kingdom of God is from you right now. The message that Jesus told His disciples to preach was that the Kingdom of Heaven is at hand.

I asked all the blind people to raise their hand. There was about fifteen hands raised. I asked them to lay their own hands over their eyes and I would pray. I cast out the spirit of blindness with the Word of God. By the use of the Words of God, I revealed to the spirit of blindness that it had no longer had any legal right to blind the people and that it had to "Let God's People GO!" (See Luke 4:18; Acts 1:8; At least 12 or 13 people testified to being healed instantly. I did the same thing in both churches for the deaf and the blind. There was a total of about 45 deaf ears and blinds eyes opened that day by the glory of God in Jesus name.

Ephesians 3:9-10
"And to make all *men* see what *is* the fellowship of the mystery, which from the beginning of the world hath been hid in God, who created all things by Jesus Christ: To the intent that now unto the principalities and powers in heavenly *places* might be known by the church the manifold wisdom of God."

We make known to the principalities and powers in the heavenly places the mystery now revealed, that Christ is not living in only one body now. He is living in millions of human bodies around the world and they all have the use of the name that's above all names, including the devils name. Now, the one problem that we have, is convincing us all that we have this kind of authority in Jesus name to cast out devils, just as Jesus told us we would.

The Holy Ghost fire was dripping from my hands as I was preaching. I could feel it but I couldn't see it.

I was walking up the Isle and preaching through a cordless microphone. I then saw a woman in a wheelchair who happened to be paralyzed from the waist down. I heard the Lord speak to me saying, "Tell two men to pick her up. She's gonna walk."

There was a stunned look on their faces. I suspect the disciples had the same look on their faces when Jesus told them to pour water into the basins to make wine. I repeated it to them more boldly, saying, "Pick her up! She's about to start walking!"

Two men picked her up by the elbows and her legs were dangling lifeless limbs. They carried her about 10 feet and then I saw them place her feet near the floor. Her feet were twisting as they did when suddenly one of her legs lifted up! And then the other! The men were still holding her tightly and she was lifting her legs in a way that looked like she never walked before.

Then when they reached the front of the church near the platform, they turned around and the woman pushed the two men aside and began walking by herself! The entire church went ballistic! People were shouting and praising the Lord! Then they started running out of the seats in the pews and running to me. I ran to the front of the church and back onto the platform. My translator calmed the people down and asked them to go back to their seats and that we would have our team come out and lay hands on everyone. I called my 16 team members together and sent them out to lay hands on the entire church. It was easy! As soon as they went towards the people, the people were running to them! The team members would lay hands on two people at a time and the people were getting healed instantly! It was so loud in the building! One woman that had a devil fell to the floor and foamed in the mouth while another was manifesting with her arms waving and screaming. We did deliverance for them quickly and they were testifying to being set free.

Jesus was in control. The devil didn't stand a chance!

Faith And Patience:

Before I laid hands on people, I taught them to not look for a feeling of healing but to look to His Promises to heal you in His name. If they were to seek the feeling, they would be disappointed. Faith was to come from the Word of God first and then the feeling of healing would follow their faith. I told them that this was the order He had given us through the record of His Word as recorded by His disciples and apostles. I explained to them that healing miracles were not always instant. Often times a healing miracle is instant, or it comes it seconds, minutes, hours, days or even at times in weeks. No matter how it comes, it will be faithful to come as long as we don't lose our faith in His Promise. I taught them that if they left the meeting that day and felt no different, it didn't mean that God was rejecting them or that they didn't have enough faith. There doesn't have to be an explanation as to why, there only needs to be the substance of faith to not let go of His Promises, like the widow who kept coming to the unjust judge. Sometimes faith requires patience and we are given many examples of that in the Word of God.

Here's one:

Hebrews 6:10-15

"For God *is* not unrighteous to forget your work and labour of love, which ye have shewed toward his name, in that ye have ministered to the saints, and do minister. And we desire that every one of you do shew the same diligence to the full assurance of hope unto the end: **That ye be not slothful, but followers of them who through faith and patience inherit the promises.** For when God made promise to Abraham, because he could swear by no greater, he swear by himself, Saying, Surely blessing I will bless thee, and multiplying I will multiply thee. And so, after he had patiently endured, he obtained the promise."

Healing miracles are generally the most likely to be instant. Financial miracles and family matters are more likely to take place over time and due diligence to do our part in seeing them come to pass. Those kind of miracles require the most patience. Healing miracles on the other hand commonly happen immediately, in seconds, minutes, hours and occasionally in days. This has been my personal experience in ministry. Nonetheless, I have seen the financial and family matters answered very quickly as well, but not always. Even the ones that don't happen instantly can be totally exciting. I have seen them all. I have seen mostly the instant, but have a lot of fun experiencing the anticipation of a soon coming miracle. It's like waiting for a gift on Christmas day. You see the gifts under the tree. You know that they are there, but you don't know what's in the box until Christmas day arrives. Being patient for a miracle is fun like that to me. I know the miracle is coming, but I may not know what minute, hour or day, but I know it's coming because I have supernatural faith in God for it to come to pass. I KNOW that He's faithful to confirm His Promises. After all, they ARE PROMISES. They are not suggestions or conjectures. They are based upon the fact of the power of His Word, not on assumptions or guesses. He never said, "I might heal you." Or "Maybe I will fulfill my Word for you." He never turned anyone away who came to Him for healing.

Name one instance in the New Testament when He denied a Jew healing when they came to Him? Even all of Syria came to Him, and they weren't Jews, yet He healed everyone from that country that needed healing. Every single one of them:

Matthew 4:23-24
"And Jesus went about all Galilee, teaching in their synagogues, and preaching the gospel of the kingdom, and healing all manner of sickness and all manner of disease among the people. And his fame went throughout all Syria: and they brought unto him all sick people that were taken with divers diseases and torments, and those which were possessed with devils, and those which were lunatic, and those that had the palsy; and he healed them."

The Word of God Is Evidence:

The testimonies that we read about in the four Gospels and in the life of the apostle Paul are evidence that God wants to heal all who come to Him by supernatural faith. He always offered healing to people and everyone who came to Him He healed them. This is the order that we see in the four Gospels as written by Matthew, Mark, Luke and John.

We need to put our faith in the Promises of God and that includes the testimonies that we see in the four Gospels. They are evidence to us of the Will of God to heal. 17 times I found that Jesus healed all who came to Him. Not once did I find any evidence that He denied any Jew who came to Him. Not once did I find any evidence that He denied any non-Jew who came to Him.

Faith is not a feeling but the feeling of healing always follows faith:

Our faith activates His Promises for every realm of life. Jesus never said, "Do you feel healed?" He said, "Do you believe?" or "According to your faith may it be done unto you."

The action of faith is essential in activating the promises of God in our lives.

Summon the Lord. "Call Upon His Name"

Genesis 4:26
"And to Seth, to him also there was born a son; and he called his name Enos: then began men to **call upon the name of the LORD.**

1Chronicles 16:8
"Give thanks unto the LORD, **call upon his name,** make known his deeds among the people."

Psalm 99:6-7
"Moses and Aaron among his priests, and Samuel **among them that call upon his name; they called upon the LORD,** and he answered them. He spake unto them in the cloudy pillar: they kept his testimonies, and the ordinance *that* he gave them."

Psalm 105:1-2
"O give thanks unto the LORD; **call upon his name:** make known his deeds among the people. Sing unto him, sing psalms unto him: talk ye of all his wondrous works."

This is a prophecy for His Church to act upon today. This is what He told me to do and I did it every time I preached. I just talked about how awesome He is and that He's here in our midst as He promised. I spoke about testimonies of other miracles everywhere I was preaching and I always made it clear that it was in the name of Jesus Christ of Nazareth that we were gathering in. I glorified His name through personal testimonies and through testimonies of those in the Bible such as Moses, King David, the disciples and others that are written about in the Bible as a representation of His faithfulness. We are witnesses of His resurrection and in order to do that we need a credible witness. He promised to give us that credible witness.

Isaiah 12:2-4
"Behold, God *is* my salvation; I will trust, and not be afraid: for the LORD JEHOVAH *is* my strength and *my* song; he also is become my salvation. Therefore with joy shall ye draw water out of the wells of salvation. **And in that day shall ye say, Praise the LORD, call upon his name, declare his doings among the people, make mention that his name is exalted.**"

Romans 10:13
"For whosoever shall call upon the name of the Lord shall be saved."

1Corinthians 1:2
"Unto the church of God which is at Corinth, to them that are sanctified in Christ Jesus, called *to be* saints, **with all that in every place call upon the name of Jesus Christ our Lord,** both theirs and ours."

"To call upon the name of the Lord." This is a very powerful promise of God. **The word "call" in Hebrew, means:** "to call out to (i.e. properly, address by name) … to call, call out, recite, read, cry out, proclaim … **to summon**, invite, call for, call and commission, appoint, call and endow."

There's POWER in the name of Jesus Christ our Lord and our Savior. The apostles always called upon the name of the Lord in prayer, while preaching, when praying for the sick and diseased, when raising the dead and the lame. (See more scriptures for the name of the Lord at the end of the chapter.)

Acts 3:16

"And his name through faith in his name hath made this man strong, whom ye see and know: yea, the faith which is by him hath given him this perfect soundness in the presence of you all."

Summon In A Court of Law

One of the meanings for calling upon the name of the Lord is: "To Summon."

When a person is summoned to attend a legal court, they are expected by law to attend. From the beginning, men and women have been inspired by the truth that there's power in calling upon the name of the Lord. When we call on His name, we are summoning Him, and He WILL come. This is His promise to mankind, that "whosoever shall call upon the name of the Lord shall be saved." When we call upon His name, we should expect that He has come to confirm His Word, whether we can feel His Presence or not. His promises are not activated by feelings. Jesus never asked people if they feel healed. He asked them if they believe. His Promises are activated by faith in His name.

Act 3:16

"And his name through faith in his name hath made this man strong, whom ye see and know: yea, the faith which is by him hath given him this perfect soundness in the presence of you all."

Why did Jesus ask people if they believed? It's because belief in the Promises of God are a sign that we have supernatural faith. It simply means that we have confidence in God to back up His Promises when we ask in His name, just as He promised us many times in His Word. A person strong belief, or call it, "Confidence" in the Promises of God are a true sign that they have supernatural faith. I recognized this when in China and after I came back to Canada. I learned how to see faith by peoples actions. When I saw that woman come again and again I knew she had supernatural faith and it was by her own supernatural faith that I knew she would be healed. It wasn't going to be because I had supernatural faith for her healing. I knew she had supernatural faith already by her action. That made it easy for me to stand in front of the people coming to that weekly miracle meeting and tell them that she will be healed. The only thing that would stopped her from being healed would have been herself. If she gave up after one or two or even four meetings, she may have lost her supernatural faith.

Jesus said: "For where two or three are gathered together in my name, there am I in the midst of them." (See Matthew 18:20) He said He will come when we summon Him by His name, so He WILL come. That's a fact. His Words are Truth and no lie. We can rest on that fact in every realm of our lives. By our action of coming together in His name, we are summoning Him to come. You could say it like this, if we want to experience the Lord in His fullness in our midst, all we need to do is gather together in His name. He WILL be there, whether we feel it or not. His Promises are faction not fiction. His Word is His bond, or as He showed me many years ago, that His Word is solid and un-moveable like an oak tree.

Raising the Lame in the Name of the Lord:

Peter and John had told a man who had been lame from his birth to stand up and walk in Jesus name. When they were questioned about what they had done, Peter exalted the name of Jesus:

Acts 3:16
"And his name through faith in his name hath made this man strong, whom ye see and know: yea, the faith which is by him hath given him this perfect soundness in the presence of you all."

Acts 3:6-7
"Then Peter said, Silver and gold have I none; but such as I have give I thee: **In the name of Jesus Christ of Nazareth rise up and walk.** And he took him by the right hand, and lifted *him* up: and immediately his feet and ankle bones received strength."

This is very powerful, but there's still a question for most of us who are trying to learn how to successfully heal lame. That question is: "I don't know anyone who is lame, so how would that apply to my life?" Most of us also secretly hope that we would never be put in the position of having to pray for someone who is lame, because we expect that we will have no success. The same thing goes for praying for the deaf, blind or seriously ill cancer patient.

Most of us, including myself, learn best with small steps. Some of us get put in a position of the worst case scenario at an early point, but usually not. One of the best ways I have personally learned the power of healing, is to apply it to myself or someone you're close to. I built my faith in the Word of God before applying it. That's the best first step. Once we have done that much, we can then begin to ask the Lord to "graciously" introduce us to our first miracle. It may be for ourselves, or another individual. Personally, I found that reading testimonies from good healing evangelists built my confidence quickly when I was ready to pray for someone to be healed. Testimonies are contagious. They radiate with the most contagious kind of faith. I harnessed the power of the testimony by always asking the people to testify to their miracle. When I was at the last church before leaving back to Canada, I was standing in front of a crowd of about 700 people. That was the first of two churches I preached in that day. While I was preaching, I called upon the leader who had come with six other leaders to meet me. She was the one who had several serious diseases killing her body and was miraculously healed. I asked her to come up front and testify to her healing miracle. I had given her no warning that I would invite her to share because I found that when giving people warning, they get nervous about how they will share it and wish they never said yes to sharing. I want people to feel confident and bold when sharing, so I invite them and don't give them any time to feel too nervous.

When she came up and shared her testimony, she did very well and it made a deep impression on the crowd, setting the stage for the Lord to present the truth as presented in the Gospels. People find it easier to believe after they see the miracle happen, so that's why I believe in having exposure to miracles as the best form of building the faith we already have. If there's a powerful healing evangelist coming somewhere close enough for you to go, then bring someone who needs a big miracle. Help them to get the healing they need. Encourage them with the Word of God that you know. This is how one of the most powerful healing evangelists had his beginnings. Smith Wigglesworth would bring many sick and lame people to where he knew miracles were happening. The people would get healed and he would go get more every week. On one occasion the leaders who were praying for the sick and lame had to leave town to do some other ministry temporarily, and asked Smith to pray for the people to be healed while they were away. He didn't want to. He was too scared to pray for people himself, but he reluctantly gave in and was amazed that when he laid hands on the sick, they were healed! Smith continued in the healing ministry from the age of 40-80. He died in 1947.

Matthew 4:23
"And Jesus went about all Galilee, teaching in their synagogues, and preaching the gospel of the kingdom, and healing all manner of sickness and all manner of disease among the people."

Matthew 4:24
"And his fame went throughout all Syria: and they brought unto him all sick people that were taken with divers diseases and torments, and those which were possessed with devils, and those which were lunatic, and those that had the palsy; and he healed them."

Not Only Jesus & The Apostles Did Miracles In His Name:

Mark 9:35-40
"And he sat down, and called the twelve, and saith unto them, If any man desire to be first, *the same* shall be last of all, and servant of all. And he took a child, and set him in the midst of them: and when he had taken him in his arms, he said unto them, Whosoever shall receive one of such children in my name, receiveth me: and whosoever shall receive me, receiveth not me, but him that sent me. And John answered him, saying, Master, we saw one casting out devils in thy name, and he followeth not us: and we forbad him, because he followeth not us. But Jesus said, Forbid him not: **for there is no man which shall do a**

miracle in my name, that can lightly speak evil of me. For he that is not against us is on our part."

Mark 16:17-18
"And these signs shall follow them that believe; In my name shall they cast out devils; they shall speak with new tongues; They shall take up serpents; and if they drink any deadly thing, it shall not hurt them; they shall lay hands on the sick, and they shall recover."

"These signs shall follow them that believe." Jesus didn't say: "These signs shall follow only the apostles", or "These signs shall only follow the elders, or pastors, or deacons." He said: "Them that believe." There is so much fear about being deceived when it comes to miracles. It was the same in Jesus' day too. They accused Him of casting out devils by the power of the devil. Today, churches all over the world are still accusing Believers of casting out devils by the power of the devil. They are giving the devil more credit than Jesus.

Another Seventy Are Sent:

Jesus also sent another seventy and they went and healed the sick and cast out devils in the power of His name.

Luke 10:1,2,9, 17-19
"After these things **the Lord appointed other seventy also, and sent them two and two before his face into every city and place,** whither he himself would come. Therefore said he unto them, The harvest truly *is* great, but the labourers *are* few: pray ye therefore the Lord of the harvest, that he would send forth labourers into his harvest...... And heal the sick that are therein, and say unto them, The kingdom of God is come nigh unto you...... And the seventy returned again with joy, saying, Lord, even the devils are subject unto us through thy name. And he said unto them, I beheld Satan as lightning fall from heaven. Behold, I give unto you power to tread on serpents and scorpions, and over all the power of the enemy: and nothing shall by any means hurt you."

He sent seventy more **two and two before his face into every city and place,** whither he himself would come. Wow!! That's a lot more than just the twelve, which many claim were the only one's who were the sent ones. And it wasn't just once that He sent the seventy. He sent them to "Every city and place, whither He himself would come." That's everywhere! We should practice the same things. This is how I preached in China. I would bring the team with me and they would minister with me and after I left, they went out and continued the work in other villages and cities. We should learn to trust people, not just trust ourselves. When we trust people, we bring out the best in them.

Matthew 18:19-20
"Again I say unto you, That if two of you shall agree on earth as touching any thing that they shall ask, it shall be done for them of my Father which is in heaven. **For where two or three are gathered together in my name, there am I in the midst of them.**" This is why Jesus sent them out two by two. It's because there's power in agreement in the heavenly places on earth.

Healing Deceptions:

I know there are miracle deceptions, but not all of them are a deception. It's easy to know the difference if we do our homework. I discovered many deceptive miracle missions in China. They are operating in the name of Jesus, but it's another Jesus. It's not the same Jesus as the Bible teaches about. It's a good idea to learn about what other so called Christian Churches believe, so that we can recognize the deception when it's presented to us. There's many books available in Christian book stores that describe what the other church doctrines are.

The Seventh Day Adventist Deception:

Seventh Day Adventist is the largest deceptive church I found in China. Not only are they the largest deceptive church in China, but they may very well be the largest church in China. One of their deceptive claims is that the dead appear to them with halo's over their head. These spirits claim to be the true saints of God. They claim that they were not believers when they died, but got saved after death and were then assigned by the Lord to take the Gospel to the world. They are deceiving spirits that deliver heresies that contradict the Word of God. They say that they are the true saints of God and have been sent to roam over the earth and reveal the truth to people. The false Prophetess, Ellen White, one of the cofounders of the SDA's, has written more books than the Bible itself with teachings that were inspired by these dead saints.

Many of these SDA's also have massive healing line ups after church on Sundays. People get healed too, but I doubt they ever see the dead raised or deaf ears and blind eyes open. I knew several SDA preachers there and they tried creeping into my ministry and deceive my people. They meet on Saturdays in their own churches and on Sundays, they visit the Christian churches, blend in, make friends, act like true dedicated Christians and then teach the false teachings to unsuspecting Believers. They hold celebrations in their churches on special holidays and invite all the Christian churches to participate by sending a team to do a show. They will spend all day in the church and have food, singing, performances and friendship. Many real Christians get hooked and feel cared for and appreciated and leave their churches for the SDA's through this form of evangelism in China.

When we stick to the Word of God, and study through good solid sources, that have the right doctrines, then we can feel safe.

Faith activates the promises of God:

This is why Jesus said to individuals who were healed, "Thy faith hath made thee whole." (See Mark 5:34; 10:52; Luke 8:48) In simpler words, it means, "Your faith in God has activated the promise of salvation for your body to be made whole because He is the Saviour of your body." It can also be said like this: "Because you believe the will of God to heal you, He is not restricted from healing (saving) you, which is what He came to do for all who come to Him by faith."

The very word, "Saved", as used by Jesus, in the Greek means:
sōzō
sode'-zo
From a primary word σως sos (contraction for the obsolete σαος saos, "safe"); to *save*, that is, *deliver* or *protect* (literally or figuratively): - heal, preserve, save (self), do well, be (make) whole.

Salvation is one of the most powerful Words in the Gospels. It's the word, "sozo" and is pronounced as: *sode'-zo*

It's a Word of God and when declared over a person, we are releasing it's power over them. I often will declare it over a person when I lay hands on them for healing, saying, "I declare that you sozo life to your whole body in Jesus name. Amen." His Words are spirit and they are life.

He is sovereign, but He will not go against our free will. Lots of what God does in our lives is based upon our response to Him. Even if we make trouble for our lives, He is there to save us. He is always looking out for us. He is always at work in our lives to shape, mold and prepare us for our destiny. He gives each one of us talents according to our abilities. (See Matthew 25:14-27) Everything we go through is a required preparation meant to give us the needed ability to apply those talents at the God-given timing. He chose the family that would raise us. That was before we were born. There's a purpose for everything, including our mistakes. "We know that all things work together for good to them that love God, to them who are called according to his purpose." (Romans 8:28)

The only thing standing between us and our healing, is US. The Lord already paid for our sicknesses and diseases 2,000 years ago. There's nothing more He can do to remove them from us. He did all that needs to be done. Now it's up to us to know the truth of what He did for us and activate it by faith. If we don't know the promises of God for us, we can't activate them in our lives.

I want to make it clear, that as ministers of the Gospel, we never make people feel like failures if they don't succeed in receiving a healing. We don't want to make them feel like they want to hide in the back of the church now because they didn't get healed. Sometimes healings take a long time and sometimes the people with the greatest faith to see others healed when they pray for them still struggle to get their own healing at times.

I had one woman who was on my ministry team who came to get healed but didn't get it but she was excited to see others healed and would go out and share the gospel every day in the market places and lay hands on those needing healing. Many that she laid hands on were instantly healed and came unto salvation through Christ. Her husband wasn't interested in church but she convinced him to come to my weekly Tuesday miracle meeting. He approached me after the meeting and said that he couldn't hear a word I said even though I had a microphone and speaker. When I asked him why he found it so difficult, he told me that he was totally deaf in his left ear and had only partial hearing in his right ear. Then I understood that he needed a miracle. I laid my hand over his left ear and commanded it to open in Jesus name. He didn't hear any difference so I did it again and then had my translator test it, and before she tested it, the Lord spoke a word to her, saying, "I'm opening his ears so that he can hear My Gospel and believe." She was so excited that she heard this word from the Lord that she was explaining how He showed this to her. I then said to her, "Well, praise the Lord! Test his hearing now." She had forgotten to actually test his hearing. When she tested it, he could hear clearly! So I did the same for his right ear and it opened the same as the left one. The man's wife was not yet healed herself, but she was so excited that the Lord had healed her husband, because now he was very interested in coming to church and the meetings. She no longer had to persuade him. He became one of my ministry team members as well. Many people were saved upon the knowledge and testimony of this man's ears being healed.

I will never forget the woman who had been given 3 months to live due to cancer. She heard his testimony, and came to a house meeting in another city. The house was full with about 50 people. I didn't hardly remember laying hands on her but I do remember hearing that she was sent to the hospital emergency about 2 weeks later. She was in so much pain so they thought the cancer was killing her. They had her tested in the emergency and found no cancer at all! She accepted Jesus as Lord and Savior and began witnessing for Him sharing her testimony and leading others to salvation through Him. When she got up in front of churches to share her testimony, she was smiling so much and so happy for what the Lord had done for her.

The Woman With Who Had An Issue Of Blood:

There was a woman who had an issue of blood who was waiting for Jesus to come to her city so she could be healed. (See Luke 8:43-48) She had faith to be healed by touching His garment. She must have heard what everyone was talking about, saying, "Everyone who touches His garment is healed." (See Matthew 14:36) This testimony grew faith in her heart. She said those words to herself, saying, "If I only touch His garment, I will be healed." (See Mark 5:28) Then once she put action to her faith, she activated the promises of God to heal her through the Messiah. (See also Matthew 14:36; Mark 6:56).

Jesus said to her, "Daughter, thy faith hath made thee whole; go in peace, and be whole of thy plague." (See Mark 5:35) The word "whole" as used here is actually two different Greek words. One of those words is the Word Sozo and the other is Se which means: "thee, thou, X thy house." The first time I saw this second word ever used by Jesus was when I was preaching in China. I see that Jesus was telling her that her faith not only saved her but her family also! Wow! Praise the Lord! I began preaching it and other scriptures throughout the Bible that show the Lord's salvation for our families. At that point in time, many families began coming to salvation through Christ. What we preach we reach! Thank You Jesus!

The second time Jesus uses the word "whole" in this sentence, it has another meaning in the Greek which is also wonderful. It's the Greek word "hugiēs" and means: "*healthy*, that is, *well* (in body); figuratively *true* (in doctrine): - sound, whole. Increase."

The Feeling Of Healing Will Follow Your Faith:

Faith comes first. Faith is based upon the fact of God's Promises to us. Then the feeling of healing always follows our faith, because

God's faithful and always confirms His Promises Positively. He's not a neglectful parent. This woman had faith before Jesus came to her city because of the testimonies she had heard about Him, but without the action, she was left in her condition. She knew that she would be healed when she touched Jesus' garment, because everyone who touched Him was healed. Once she put action to her faith, it was manifested in her body. Her faith with action activated the promises of God for salvation in her body. When she put action to her faith, the power of the Kingdom of Heaven that Jesus was hosting, was released and made her body whole. By her faith, she was reaching into the heavenly places, touching the riches in the glory and partaking of the spiritual blessings there. (See Ephesians 1:3; Philippians 4:19)

Romans 9:23-24
"And that he might make known the riches of his glory on the vessels of mercy, which he had afore prepared unto glory, Even us, whom he hath called, not of the Jews only, but also of the Gentiles?"

Ephesians 1:17-23
"That the God of our Lord Jesus Christ, the Father of glory, may give unto you the spirit of wisdom and revelation in the knowledge of him: The eyes of your understanding being enlightened; that ye may know what is the hope of his calling, and **what the riches of the glory of his inheritance in the saints, And what *is* the exceeding greatness of his power to us-ward who believe, according to the working of his mighty power, Which he wrought in Christ, when he raised him from the dead, and set *him* at his own right hand in the heavenly places,** Far above all principality, and power, and might, and dominion, and every name that is named, not only in this world, but also in that which is to come: And hath put all *things* under his feet, and gave him *to be* the head over all *things* to the church, Which is his body, the fullness of him that filleth all in all."

Ephesians 3:16-17
"That he would grant you, **according to the riches of his glory,** to be strengthened with might by his Spirit in the inner man; That Christ may dwell in your hearts by faith; that ye, being rooted and grounded in love."

Colossians 1:26-27

"*Even* the mystery which hath been hid from ages and from generations, but now is made manifest to his saints: To whom God would make known **what *is* the riches of the glory of this mystery among the Gentiles; which is Christ in you, the hope of glory.**" The glory is in us, in the kingdom of God within us. All that we need in Christ is in us.

Damaged Goods Recall:

Jesus promised us that He will answer every prayer that we pray in His name and that includes asking to receive the healing He already paid for. If you buy something from the store, take it home and open it, and find that it's damaged, you will return it to the store for a refund. We are the damaged goods, and God, who is the manufacturer, is recalling all damaged goods so that He can repair and restore them to the original blueprint.

Great Faith:

Is there different levels of faith? Absolutely! Jesus addressed this at different times. He had said to His disciples: "O ye of little faith." On another occasion, He rebuked them, saying: "Where is your faith!" When a centurion came to Him asking prayer for his servant, Jesus said He would come to pray for him to be healed. The centurion said, "Speak the word only and my servant shall be healed... And Jesus said unto the centurion, Go thy way; and as thou hast believed, so be it done unto thee. And his servant was healed in the selfsame hour." (See Matthew 8:8, 13)

According to Jesus, the centurion had "Great faith". Why did he have such Great Faith? It's because he was a man of great authority and understood the power of a name. He gave commandments to his officers and they obeyed without question. He quickly recognized this same sort of authority successfully being exercised through Jesus, and knew that upon His Word, the sickness would depart from the servant as soon as Jesus commanded it to be so. It was this man's life experience that prepared him to be so open and understanding of Jesus authority.

Today, disrespect of authority is a problem that affects peoples lives spiritually. If they don't understand authority, how will they understand the authority and power of the name of Jesus Christ? It seems that a lot of people today would really benefit from spending a few years in the military, so they can learn about true authority, respect and responsibility. I'm speaking as a Canadian. There are many countries around the world that have a much stronger culture than Canada does. This is part of our problem in North America. We lack culture. That's not to say that all cultures nurture the best attitude in people, but many have good and strong values regarding authority, respect and responsibility.

Jesus Our Burden Bearer:

Jesus came to be our burden bearer. He said, "Come unto me and I will give you rest." (Matt. 11:28-30) What more do we need to know? He came to take every sorrow, grief, sickness, disease, calamity and poverty. He became poor so we could become rich. He took all the sicknesses, diseases and poverty of the world upon Himself so that we could be free from it. He's standing at the door knocking and waiting for us to open it so that He can come in bearing His gifts for our salvation in every realm of our lives. There's nothing we need to do to receive it. Our good works don't earn us first place in line. We receive it by faith in His name alone. There's no second place in line when we walk by faith. Faith always places us in the first place.

"Would You Like To Be Healed?"

He comes to us saying, "Would you like to be healed? Would you like to walk again? Would you like to receive your hearing back? How about your vision? How about your children? Or your business?" And we respond saying, "Yes Lord! Thank You Jesus!" And as we follow Him, He does it just as He promised. This is the truth and it's very simple. "Ye have not because you ask not." (See James 4:2B) One day in 2012, back here in Canada, when I was sitting in a coffee shop in a local mall, all the tables were occupied and a middle eastern gentleman asked if he could share my table with me. I agreed. He began speaking to me, and when I replied, he could not hear me because he was nearly deaf. I asked him, "Would you like to hear?" The man said, "Yes, of course. How is that possible?" I told Him that Jesus could heal his ears. He didn't want me to pray for him but I told him that it was too late. I already prayed for him in my mind and that he would wake up with restored hearing the next morning. He said he wouldn't believe it unless he saw it happen. I saw him in the same mall 2 weeks later and he told me that it happened just as I said. His ears were opened. I tested his hearing and saw that it was true. Jesus healed the man.

Another time, in 2013, I was sitting in a mall food court with a couple of friends. I saw someone limping while they walked by and I left my friends to go talk to the person to see if I can pray for them. I interrupted the girl who was limping and she could not hear me, because it turned out that she was partly deaf. She was wearing hearing aides and needed to read my lips to understand me. When I realized this, I said hi to her, introduced myself to her and apologized because I didn't realize that she was deaf. I then asked her a simple question. I said, "Would you like to be able to hear without hearing aides?" And she looked at me with a bent face and a Big question mark. So I asked her again, "Would you like to have perfect hearing so that you don't need hearing aides anymore?" She said to me, "How can that happen?" I then said, "Jesus can touch you and heal your ears when I pray for it. Would you like that?" She looked at me funny again with her head bent sideways, then said, "What will you do?" I replied, "I will just put my hand over your ear and pray to Jesus to heal it and open it for you." Then after hesitating for several more seconds, she agreed. She removed her hearing aides and I laid the palm of my left hand over hear right ear. I asked Jesus to place His hands on her ears and open them. I then commanded the ears to open. I removed my hand and spoke the word, "Open!" in one ear and then the other ear. Her eyes got Big! I began speaking to her and asked her if she could hear. She was shocked and said, "Yes! I can hear you! Can you talk some more?" So I talked more to her and she was so amazed and wanted to know how I did it. I then asked if she would like to come meet my friends and share with them what happened. She did, and my friends were excited to hear the testimony. They talked with her and tested her ears and she could hear them well as they spoke together. I have done this other times as well, with the same success. Praise the Lord! He is still doing the same things today as He did 2,000 years ago!

Salvation For The Whole Family:

I preached "Salvation for your whole family!" and they received this and entire families were getting saved. They believed the words of God concerning all His riches in glory. It's not complicated at all. We simply need to become like children and believe every promise of God, and by our faith in His Promises, we are activating them in our lives. There are in fact many promises in the Bible for the salvation of our whole family, and once we begin to activate them by our faith, we see them get saved.

Acts 16:30-31
"And brought them out, and said, Sirs, what must I do to be saved? And they said, **Believe on the Lord Jesus Christ, and thou shalt be saved, and thy house.**"

God receives glory when His Promises are activated and brought to pass in our lives.

2Corinthians 1:20
"For all the promises of God in him *are* yea, and in him Amen, unto the glory of God by us."

Faith Sometimes Requires Patience:

Hebrews 6:12
"Be not slothful, but followers of them **who through faith and patience inherit the promises.**"

Sometimes the healing occurs instantly. This is not the result in every case. Sometimes healing occurs in seconds, minutes, hours, days or even weeks. Jesus guaranteed us that when we plant the Word seeds into our heart, they will grow. (See Mark. 4:26) So just plant the Words of God into your heart, and while your asleep or while you're awake, they will be growing and when they bring forth fruit, it will be time for a harvest of the promises of God in your life. (See Mark. 4:29) We can be like the centurion, who said to Jesus, "Speak the word only, and my servant shall be healed." (See Matthew 8:8) Eight verses later, in the book of Matthew, we read of Jesus casting "out devils with his word, and healed

143

all that were sick." (See Matthew 8:16) Jesus overcame with His Word, in His Father's name. He sent us to do it exactly the same way. Once we or someone else who has the faith speaks the Word of God over our condition, we just need to allow the Word of God work in us by coming into agreement with it. We give power to the very thing we come into agreement with. We give power to the Word of God when we come into agreement with it. It's the same as the Lord saying, "Let there be light." The word "Let" in the Hebrew, means: "allow", "give permission". When we agree with His Word, we are giving Him permission to operate in us by the Sword of His Word, in the authority and power of His name. By our agreement with His Word, we have enacted it's power to operate on us. He comes to us, and says, "Would you like to walk?" or, "Would you like to be healed from your cancer?" or, "Would you like to see or hear again?" He is looking for our permission. He is looking for our agreement with His Promise, which is His Word. Once we agree with it, it begins it's procedure in making us whole. This is what happened to the woman with the issue of blood. She had heard the Word of God that Jesus was preaching by some of His disciples and she came into agreement with it. By coming into agreement with it, she was germinating those Word seeds. She had heard that all who touch the hem of His garment are healed and she kept telling herself, "If I may but touch his garment, I shall be whole." (See Matthew 9:21) We just need to be patient and not lose our faith, lest Jesus say to us, "Where is your faith? What happened to it? Where did you leave it?"

Matthew 18:19-20
"Again I say unto you, That if two of you shall agree on earth as touching any thing that they shall ask, it shall be done for them of my Father which is in heaven. For where two or three are gathered together in my name, there am I in the midst of them."

I Have Been Healed Many Times, In Different Ways:

I have been healed so many times by the hand of the Lord. Each time my faith rises to a new level. I am not just preaching this. I experience it myself. I had warts on my feet for about 10 years before I felt faith for them to die by the power of the name of Jesus Christ. I had seen others healed when I had prayed for them, but when I prayed for myself, there was no result. I had been to the doctor several times for them and she tried freezing them off the last time I visited her. Then I met a preacher in a Walmart. He was in the photo's line up getting some film developed from healing testimonies in one of his healing crusades. I didn't know who he was but we started talking about it in the line-up. He invited me for lunch and then to his crusade. For the first time in my life, I felt faith for my own healing. I laid hands on my feet while I was still in my seat. He prayed for everyone and I felt no change at all. Two weeks later, all the warts died, turned jet black and fell off my feet and were sitting in a pile in the toe of my socks. They quarter and dime sized. There was over 25 of them. It was a tremendous miracle to me, even though it took two weeks to happen. All that time, I felt faith that they were coming off, even though I didn't feel any physical change in my feet when he prayed at the crusade. I just kept praising the Lord for healing me all day every day during that two weeks. I was also reading over the preachers healing scripture brochure throughout the day and proclaiming those promises for me. The Word took root in my heart and brought forth the miracle.

They are all awesome and powerful if we can see them as a gift from God, no matter how they come. Jesus didn't always heal people the same way and He hasn't changed. When the 10 lepers came to Him to be healed, He told them go to the priest and tell him what the Lord had done for them. They obeyed the Lord and began walking to tell the priest about what the Lord had done for them before they were even healed. It was their obedience in faith to go do what the Lord instructed them to do that activated and manifested the healing in their bodies.

Luke 17:12
"And as he entered into a certain village, there met him ten men that were lepers, which stood afar off: And they lifted up their voices, and said, Jesus, Master, have mercy on us. And when he saw them, he said unto them, **Go shew yourselves unto the priests. And it came to pass, that, as they went, they were cleansed.**"

This kind of miracle, I call a seconds miracle. They were healed within seconds of putting action to their faith. I had a similar word from the Lord when in China. There was a 29 year old Chinese girl who had a visitation from a tall devil that looked like a man. He was at the foot of her bed holding chains in his hands and told her that he was going to chain her up and kill her before the Chinese new year. The Chinese new year was 2 weeks away. They had told their friend who happened to be one of my main team members. They asked her if she would invite me to come to their home and pray for the girl. Four of us went to visit the girl. It was about 2 hours drive by bus and when we got there the Lord told me how to begin. I had a small music box with me and we played worship music and sang praise and worship around the girls bed. Then the Lord had us read victory Bible stories over the girl.

The girl was bound by the chains in the spirit realm and could not move. She couldn't even open her mouth to eat, drink or speak during that two weeks. Where faith is, we always please God. (Heb. 11:6) **He hears us when we pray by faith because faith is based upon His promises.** Unbelief and Doubt are not.

1John 5:14
"And this is the confidence that we have in Him, that, if we ask any thing **according to his will (His Word/Promises),** he heareth us."

This is powerful! When we ask according to His will, he then hears us. If we are not asking according to His will, He does not hear us. So how to do know His will? His Word is His will. It reveals His will. His Word is His promise to us. So it's super important that we find His will in His word and ask according to it. Then we will see His hand stretch out in our midst and do what we requested. This is true for you and for all His believers.

Now, let's begin by taking a look at one very powerful promise of God that we can hook up with and activate in our lives by faith.

Matthew 8:16, 17
"When the even was come, they brought unto him many that were possessed with devils: and he cast out the spirits with his word, and healed all that were sick: That it might be fulfilled which was spoken by Esaias the prophet, saying, Himself took our infirmities, and bare out sicknesses."

Here we go. Let's break down this promise of God as given through His prophet. First of all, He cast out devils with His Word. His Word is the promises and prophecies that were spoken of Him. I discovered the power of casting out devils with the Word of God when I was living in China. I had never had to deal with casting out devils in Canada before going to China. I had no experience with it so the first time a person was brought to me that needed deliverance, I didn't know how to respond. That meant I didn't have faith to cast out devils due to my lack of knowledge about it. Once I learned the way it was done, I had lots of faith. I was full of confidence for it and then many were brought to me for deliverance and I saw them delivered and filled with the presence of the Holy Spirit.

I would declare the words of God concerning the persons freedom from death, sickness, disease and all devils and the people would be set free. It was fast, effective and very easy to do. There was very little manifestations of the devils because I could normally deal with them according to the Word before they could have a chance to speak through the person and curse me with words of death. If a devil would manifest, I would boldly tell it to shut up in Jesus name and it did. I would bind the devil from making a show through the person and it would be bound and couldn't move anymore, but sometimes it tried.

His "Word" also speaks of the law, which was written about Him. (Heb. 10:7; Matt. 5:17; Lk. 16:16) It was written about Him because the law was based upon the sin problem of mankind and Jesus was the solution to that problem. Jesus is the Lamb of God who came to take away the sins of the world. (John 1:29). He fulfilled all the law and the prophets. He didn't destroy them. The law of God was required to be fulfilled before mankind could be forgiven and healed. Once it was fulfilled in the Old Testament in accordance with the requirements, then the people could be forgiven and healed. The problem with the Old Testament law, is that it couldn't remit sins. It only brought forgiveness of sins and healing to the body. Jesus had to come to fulfill all the law once and for all so that the sacrifices of animals didn't have to continue year after year. Only through Christ do we receive remission of sins. We are not only forgiven, but washed clean from our sins because of the blood of Jesus Christ that was shed, and taken to heaven, and placed upon the mercy seat, in the true Holy Place in heaven. This sacrifice never needs to be repeated. It's been fulfilled.

In the law, there was exposure of sin and the solution was the sacrifice of a lamb, and in some cases, other animals were used. It would lift burdens of guilt for sin and bring healing and rest to the people. That's what Jesus came to do for us, not only as the Lamb of God and High Priest, but as our Sheppard. Psalm 23

Psalm 23:1-6
"The LORD is my shepherd; I shall not want. He maketh me to lie down in green pastures: he leadeth me beside still waters. He restoreth my soul: he leadeth me in the paths of righteousness for his name's sake. Yea, though I walk through the valley of the shadow of death, I will fear no evil: for thou art with me; thy rod and thy staff comfort me. Thou prepares a table before me in the presence of mine enemies: thou anointest my head with oil; my cup runneth over. Surely goodness and mercy shall follow me all the days of my life: and I will dwell in the house of the LORD for ever."

We hear Jesus making reference to this and other promises when He says:

Matthew 11:28
"Come unto me, all ye that labour and are heavy laden, and I will give you rest. Take my yoke upon you, and learn of me; for I am meek and lowly in heart: and ye shall find rest unto your souls. For my yoke is easy, and my burden is light."

The sacrifices were done by the priest of the law and only the High Priest could go into the holy places with a sacrifice for the whole nation. That's speaking of Jesus, who came as the Great High Priest and the Lamb of God who came to take away the sins of the world. (See Jn. 1:29)

The Authority of Sickness, Disease, Poverty and Calamities:

Sin was the cause of sickness, disease, and other curses according to the law. (See Deut. 28:15-67) Sin was the authority of sickness and disease. If there was no sin, then sickness and disease wouldn't have any authority to condemn mankind. Jesus removed the sin and thereby stripped sickness and disease of it's authority. Therefore, it has no legal right to condemn those who are saved. The law brought condemnation for sin by cursing mankind with sickness and disease as a form of condemnation, but Jesus took that condemnation upon Himself, by suffering the punishment for sin according to the law.

Galatians 3:13
"Christ hath redeemed us from the curse of the law, being made a curse for us: for it is written, Cursed is every one that hangeth on a tree."

Colossians 2:12-15
"Buried with him in baptism, wherein ye are risen with him through the faith of the operation of God, who hath raised him from the dead. And you, being dead in your sins and the uncircumcision of your flesh, hath he quickened together with him, having forgiven you all trespasses (offense, sin); Blotting out the handwriting of ordinances (the laws) that was against us, which was contrary to us (opposed, against us), and took it out of the way, nailing it to his cross; (He nailed the law to his cross) And having spoiled (separated from us) principalities (magistrate of darkness) and powers (authorities, jurisdiction), he made a shew (example) of them openly, triumphing over them in it (in the victory of His Cross)."

Jesus came according to the law.
Jesus suffered according to the law.
Jesus fulfilled the requirements of the law.
As the Lamb of God and High Priest, He made an offering to God the Father according to all the laws requirements for the sins of the whole world.
Jesus overcame the principalities and powers of the dark regions.
He overcame sin and death.
He over came condemnation.
He placed them under His feet.
He gave us His authority over them through the use of His name.
He made them subject unto us through His name. They must obey us in His name. When we command them to leave a person, it's a demand, not an option. We use the Word of God which is the sword of the Spirit. It causes torment on the devils when we do. (See

Matthew 8:29

"And, behold, they cried out, saying, What have we to do with thee, Jesus, thou Son of God? art thou come hither to torment us before the time?"

The Words of God bring torment on devils. That's why they complained to Jesus whenever He came.

All power in heaven and earth was given to Jesus through His victory. It means that it was removed from the dark regions. They were stripped of all authority and power. They exercise authority and power they don't have. Through the name of Jesus we have the authority over them. They are subject unto us in His name. They complained whenever Jesus came around, and when we know the power of the name and are walking in the baptism of the Holy Ghost and fire, they will complain when we come too. The religious people will not like you. They will feel agitated when you are around. People who are involved in witchcraft will feel agitated when you're around because the spirit guides that are with them will be shaking in their boots. They will want to hiss like a cat in your presence.

Matthew 5:17

"Think not that I am come to destroy the law, or the prophets: I am not come to destroy, but to fulfil."

When Jesus died on the cross, Death had one problem. Jesus Himself had no sin, so death could not hold Him in the grave. Death's authority was sin and Jesus had no sin. (See 2Corinthians 5:21) Death didn't realize that the sin that placed Jesus on the cross was the sin of the world. He was a spotless Lamb, without wrinkle or blemish. He followed the law 100% in his crucifixion. He fulfilled all that was written concerning Himself in the law and the prophets and satisfied the Father in heaven. Once the price was paid, He was free and preached to the saints waiting in Paradise for the coming King. He released them from the grave and 500 of them rose from the dead and walked about and gave witness to Christ. The rest of them ascended as a spirit and soul into heaven.

Now because Jesus took away the sins of the world, the world is free from the condemnation of the law of sin and death, as long as we come to the Lord Jesus Christ by faith in Him believing that He is Lord and that He died and rose from the dead for our sins.

Scriptures for Jesus Healing ALL who come to Him:

1. **Matthew 4:23**
   "Healing all manner of sickness and disease among the people."
2. **Matthew 4:24** "Diverse diseases, torments, possessed, lunatic, palsy, and he healed them."
3. **Matthew 8:16** "many that were possessed with devils: ... and he healed all that were sick ..."
4. **Matthew 12:15** "Great multitudes followed him, and he healed them all."
5. **Matthew 14:14** "He was moved with compassion, and he healed them all."
6. **Matthew 15:30** "Great multitudes came to him, lame, blind, dumb, maimed, many others: he healed them."
7. **Matthew 19:2** "Great multitudes followed him; and he healed them there."
8. **Matthew 21:14** "The blind and the lame came to him, and he healed them."
9. **Luke 4:40** "They that had any sick with diseases brought them to him, he laid his hands on every one and healed them."
10. **Luke 6:18** "They that were vexed with unclean spirits: and they were healed."
11. **Luke 6:19** "and the whole multitude sought to touch him; for there went virtue out of him and healed them all."
12. **Luke 9:11** "And the people, when they knew it, followed him: and he received them, and spoke unto them of the kingdom of God, and healed them that had need of healing."
13. **Mark 6:56** "They laid the sick in the streets, and besought him that they might touch if it were the border of his garment: and any as touched him were made whole."
14. **Matthew 14:36** "And besought him that they might only touch the hem of his garment: and as many as touched were made perfectly whole."

15. **Acts 5:16** "bringing sick folks, and them which were vexed with unclean spirits: and they were healed every one."

16. **Acts 10:38** "How God anointed Jesus of Nazareth with the Holy Ghost and with power: who went about doing good, and healing all that were oppressed of the devil. For God was with him (means: the kingdom of God was with him - and it's now with us as it was with Him)."

17. **Acts 28:9** "So when this was done, others also, which had diseases in the island, came, and were healed."

Scriptures for Jesus Sending All His Disciples to Do the Same Things He Did:

John 20:21
"Then said Jesus to them again, Peace be unto you: **as my Father hath sent me, even so send I you.**" How did the Father send Him? In the Gospel according to John, we read a perfect description of it: **John 1:32** says, "And John bare record, saying, I saw the Spirit descending from heaven like a dove, and it abode (Greek: "remained") upon him." The Spirit remained upon Jesus. This is how He has called us. He confirms it again in **Acts 1:8,** saying, "And ye shall receive power after that the Holy Ghost is come upon you." It came upon the 120 disciples and they became witnesses by the demonstration of the Spirit and of power, just as Jesus had been.

Jesus further confirmed that we are called just as He was called in several places:

Luke 24:49
"And, behold, I send the promise of my Father upon you: but tarry ye in the city of Jerusalem, until ye be **endued with power from on high.**"

The Greek meaning for the word **"endued"**, as used in Luke 24:49 means: "(in the sense of sinking into a garment); to invest with clothing (literally or figuratively): - array, clothe (with), endue, have (put) on.)"

More Scriptures About The Name Of Jesus:

John 20:30-31
"And many other signs truly did Jesus in the presence of his disciples, which are not written in this book: But these are written, that ye might believe that Jesus is the Christ, the Son of God; **and that believing ye might have life through his name.**"

Acts 2:38
"Then Peter said unto them, Repent, and **be baptized every one of you in the name of Jesus Christ** for the remission of sins, and ye shall receive the gift of the Holy Ghost."

John 1:12
"But as many as received him, to them gave he power to become the sons of God, *even* **to them that believe on his name.**"

Acts 4:17-19
"But that it spread no further among the people, let us straitly threaten them, **that they speak henceforth to no man in this name.** And they called them, and commanded them **not to speak at all nor teach in the name of Jesus.** But Peter and John

Acts 4:29-31
"And now, Lord, behold their threatenings: and grant unto thy servants, that with all boldness they may speak thy word, By stretching forth thine hand to heal; and that signs and wonders may be done **by the name of thy holy child Jesus.** And when they had prayed, the place was shaken where they were assembled together; and they were all filled with the Holy Ghost, and they spoke the word of God with boldness."

Acts 5:40-42
"And to him they agreed: and when they had called the apostles, and beaten *them,* they commanded **that they should not speak in the name of Jesus,** and let them go. And they departed from the presence of the council, **rejoicing that they were counted worthy to suffer shame for his name.** And daily in the temple, and in every house, they **ceased not to teach and preach Jesus Christ.**"

In front of crowds as small as 12 people and as many as 700, this message always had signs following. When I first preached this way in an underground church in China, 5 people were healed. I had only been in China for two days, and I preached the message of His resurrection and His Presence on the earth by the Holy Ghost. There was only about 20 people in the church at that time. After preaching that first day, I went out to see the city and do some shopping. When I came back to the church later that afternoon, there was five people waiting for me there. They were in the church meeting and had waited there for hours to tell me that they had been healed in the morning service. Their faces were shining with the glory of God and they were so excited as they were all trying to tell their testimony to me at the same time. They were pointing to the parts of their bodies that were healed. One woman was bending in all directions to show me she was healed, another was jumping up and down and praising the Lord. They had never seen such miracles in their life. I preached there 5 Sundays in a row and the church grew from 20 to 60 people in that time.

One Sunday, a woman came forward from the back of the room after I was finished preaching. She boldly came up to me in front of the whole congregation and said, "Can Jesus heal me?" I said, "Yes, what do you need Him to do for you?" She said, "I'm totally deaf in my left ear and have only partial hearing in my right ear and I also have a disease in my liver." I said, "Yes, Jesus will heal you right now because He's here to do so." I then looked to the congregation and told them, "Jesus is about to open her ears. Just watch and see what the Lord will do to prove His Love and His resurrection." I placed my finger in her left ear, commanded it to open and then tested it. The woman was amazed! She said, "Yes! I can hear? But just a little bit." I said, "Ok, I will pray for the other ear and they will both open completely." So I did so, and they both opened completely. Praise the Lord! She said that she had never been to church before and came because her girlfriend had come the week before and was healed of an incurable disease in her throat. She was so amazed by her girlfriends healing because she was with her when she was diagnosed with the disease. **There's freedom in His Glory!**

John 11:25
"Jesus said unto her, **I am the resurrection, and the life:** he that believeth in me, though he were dead, yet shall he live."

Acts 1:22
"Beginning from the baptism of John, unto that same day that he was taken up from us, must one be ordained **to be a witness with us of his resurrection.**"

More Testimonies

The Cloud Of Glory Rolled Into The Living Room

I was in a Chinese house prayer meeting one time. They always have dinner together and a social time before they begin. I was invited to share with them a little regarding miracles when I was in China. During the social time, I simply said to one gentlemen, "Jesus is alive you know. He is risen from the dead and He's here now with power to heal." He had a look of surprise on his face, and then smiled and agreed with me. About 15 minutes later we all gathered in the living room to begin. There was 13 there including myself. One woman began by sharing a testimony of how the Lord had touched her the previous week. As she was sharing, I saw the cloud of glory coming into the room. I immediately interrupted her testimony, saying, "Excuse me, but I just saw the cloud of His glory coming into the room and the Lord told me that if we will welcome Him now, He will heal everyone instantly."

Everyone immediately lifted up their hands to Jesus and closed their eyes. Less than a minute later one of the Chinese men yelled out that he was healed. Then another one and one of the women next. The first man to testify was on medication for a large lump on his forearm near his elbow. It was a build-up of fluid under the skin about the size of a golf ball. He was told by the doctors it would drain in about 3 months. After the cloud of His glory came in, it disappeared instantly! The other man's knee was instantly healed. He had tears as he was sharing in amazement as to what Jesus had done. Then a woman whose hand was numb for a long time shared how she was also healed.

This all happened after I just spoke about the Kingdom of God and the fact that Jesus is alive and here just as He said He would be.

Mother And Daughter Healed From Eczema

Then another Chinese woman came over to pick up her daughter that was playing upstairs with other children. I knew her because she had come to previous house meetings I had been doing weekly for several months. She came and testified to me how her eczema on her hands was healed since I had laid hands on them in Jesus name. She then asked me to lay hands on her daughter who had eczema worse than she had it. It was on the 8 year old girls face around her mouth, on her lips, her hands and her knees. It was very painful for her. I laid hands on the little girls head and thanked Jesus for healing her. Two months later, I saw the little girl and saw that she was totally healed and very happy.

The wave of His glory creates ripples that affect many beyond our knowledge. Where these kind of works are non-existent, I doubt that the Holy Ghost has any liberty at all.

Mark 16:17-20
"And **these signs shall follow them that believe;** In my name shall they cast out devils; they shall speak with new tongues; They shall take up serpents; and if they drink any deadly thing, it shall not hurt them; they shall lay hands on the sick, and they shall recover. So then after the Lord had spoken unto them, he was received up into heaven, and sat on the right hand of God. And they went forth, and preached every where, **the Lord working with *them*, and confirming the word with signs following. Amen.**"

How The Lord Prepared Me:

The Lord prepared me with these scriptures before I went to China and by sitting in prayer in His Presence for hours daily. As I sought Him to reveal His will, He showed me these and other verses to build the needed faith in me. He then brought other ministers into my life over the years who would mentor me little by little along the way.

I had the opportunity to go on some ministry trips with a couple other preachers who were already active in healing ministry. At those times I saw lots of miracles happen. I was part of a ministry healing team and saw lots of people healed when I prayed for them. This built my courage and confidence in the Word of God. This kind of exposure I believe is very necessary in getting us prepared to go out and do it ourselves. I am expecting that as a result of this book, there will be many who will come to where I am to learn what I learned and experience what I have experienced. I am not the only person on this planet who wants to do this kind of ministry and though there are many ministers like myself, most of us have trouble finding them and making contact with them in an atmosphere that will help us reach the level of ministry we are looking for.

Exposure:

Exposure is the best way to grow into ministry and getting close to those who are already seasoned in it is the best way that I know how to appropriate the Word of God for that purpose. Just be careful because I found that sometimes they may feel threatened by the new people who come and are so excited to serve the Lord is ministry. I have been stabbed in the back by the people I looked up to more than

For many years I had studied books by other preachers who were well seasoned in the healing ministry, but I never had any great success with it until I had exposure to them and their ministries. I have found this to be true for most believers. Just reading the books is not enough. I trained 80 Chinese believers in the healing ministry for several months. That included seeing miracles done by their hands every week. During our last week meeting before I returned to Canada, they were still nervous when they went to pray for the sick and needy. Once the anointing came upon them, that nervousness left. Nonetheless, while some of them felt bold immediately and began sharing the Gospel daily, most others still needed the exposure repeatedly before they could go out and do it on their own. I believe this is one reason why many preachers today have little success with healing ministry. They're not exposed to it in Bible school yet they are expected to be experts on the topic, myself included. I went to two different Bible schools part time, but neither of them could prepare me for healing ministry. Just having a preacher visit for one week or two is not enough to prepare an entire church for healing ministry. It takes time. It takes dedication to the topic of healing. It requires lots of exposure.

I don't say this to discourage anyone. I say it to give realistic advice for those who are wishing to be active in this kind of ministry. If you aren't getting the training where you are now, then find out where you can. That's hard to do because there's very few who know how to do it and of those few, there are even fewer who want to share what they know with others. You have to start on your own by studying about healing in the Bible, then you need to pray that the Lord will give you the opportunity to begin on your own, or to find you the right person to help you.

I can honestly say that studying the Word of God for healing with the use of famous healing evangelists books is a good way to prepare yourself before getting the exposure, and while getting the exposure. I studied it for years before getting much exposure and it did me a world of good. I had the Word in my heart and mind, so when I saw it in action, I could relate to it in the Word. I was seeing the Word in action.

Some of my favorite preachers for healing ministry are:

Smith Wigglesworth
T.L. Osborne
F.F. Bosworth

If you can read some of their material, it will benefit you greatly. I believe they are some of the best authorities in the area of healing ministry. T.L. Osborne Materials will be the easiest to get access to. "The Gospel According To T.L. & Daisy" is probably the best first read for Miracle Ministry education with hundreds of testimonies and pictures included throughout the book.

Casting Out Devils - You're Protected

Ephesians 6:13-18
"Wherefore take unto you the whole armour of God, that ye may be able to withstand in the evil day, and having done all, to stand. Stand therefore, having your loins girt about with truth, and having on the breastplate of righteousness; And your feet shod with the preparation of the gospel of peace; Above all, taking the shield of faith, wherewith ye shall be able to quench all the fiery darts of the wicked. And take the helmet of salvation, and the sword of the Spirit, which is the word of God: Praying always with all prayer and supplication in the Spirit, and watching thereunto with all perseverance and supplication for all saints."

John 17:18
"As thou hast sent me into the world, even so have I also sent them into the world."

John 17:22
"And the glory which thou gavest me I have given them." The glory of the Lord is not for having fuzzy feelings. It's the very presence of the Lord Himself, in us and with us. It includes the power and authority of His name. It also includes the confirming of the Word of God as we preach it.

Mark 3:14-15

"And he ordained twelve, that they should be with him, and that he might send them forth to preach, And to have power to heal sicknesses, and to cast out devils."

Luke 10:1, 11, 17-19

"After these things the Lord appointed other seventy also, and sent them two and two before his face into every city and place, whither he himself would come." 11 "Even the very dust of your city, which cleaveth on us, we do wipe off against you: notwithstanding be ye sure of this, that the kingdom of God is come nigh unto you." 17 "And the seventy returned again with joy, saying, Lord, even the devils are subject unto us through thy name. 18 And he said unto them, I beheld Satan as lightning fall from heaven. 19 Behold, I give unto you power to tread on serpents and scorpions, and over all the power of the enemy: and nothing shall by any means hurt you."

Matthew 8:16-17

"When the even was come, they brought unto him many that were possessed with devils: and he cast out the spirits with *his* word, and healed all that were sick: That it might be fulfilled which was spoken by Esaias the prophet, saying, Himself took our infirmities, and bare *our* sicknesses."

Romans 1:16

"I am not ashamed of the gospel of Christ: for it is the power of God …"
The Gospel of Christ is the Power of God.

These above scriptures are very powerful and empowering for the Believer in the Gospel of Christ. The Holy Ghost, who is the one who reveals the Word of God to us, has led me to these scriptures many many times. He has ministered them to me in the deepest ways. It was especially when I was called into action in China that I really understood their meaning. I can teach you what I learned, but the best way for you to learn, is to experience it first hand in ministry.

Many of us have heard the preaching about the armour of God one or more times but did we really understand it? If you never experienced confronting the darkness, then you wouldn't have any true knowledge of what it means to cast out devils, tear down strongholds, or to defend other people from the darkness.

Faith is substantial to our walk and if we want to have faith for casting out devils, then we need to have it revealed to us by the Holy Ghost, not just from reading a book about someone else's experiences and understanding of it. The right teaching is necessary, but it will never give you experience, unless you are brought into the ministry field.

Matthew 8:16B
"And he cast out the spirits with his word ..."

I didn't have the revelation of this before I went to China. It was there that the Lord revealed to me how "we, His disciples, cast out devils with His Word." I had read it in the Word many times, but didn't have the revelation of it.

For example:

Jesus, when tempted by Satan in the wilderness, overcame him with the use of the Word of God. After three temptations Satan was defeated and deflated. The Word of God is the weapon of our warfare. (See 2Corinthians 10:3-6) It's called "the sword of the Spirit." When we use the Word of God in defense or offense against the darkness, it is The Sword of the Spirit of God in our mouth. Satan is literally overcome by the Word of God. Hence the reason why it was so important for it to be written concerning how Jesus cast out devils, saying, "He cast out the spirits with His word." It's no different for us. (See also Hebrews 4:12, Ephesians 6:17, John 20:21, 14:12)

Jesus came as the last Adam. Not the second Adam, but the last Adam and as the last Adam, He was and is a quickening spirit. (See 1Corinthians 15:45) The first Adam was only a living soul. Adam is not active in the earth today but Jesus Christ is. He was doing great things when He walked on the earth, and today, as a quickening spirit, He is still very active and unlimited in His work on the earth. The first Adam failed in overcoming Satan in the garden. Jesus came to complete what Adam failed to do and now that He has successfully accomplished that goal, Satan is left empty handed and without hope. The authority that Adam lost to the serpent in the garden, Jesus got back in the wilderness, leaving the serpent powerless against the church. Jesus has created a way for us in to operate in His Power and Authority in His name so that through us, He can continue to stretch forth His Mighty hand to heal, deliver, set the captives free and create New Life in families abroad.

I was confronted with people needing deliverance sometimes 2-3 times each week for the last seven months that I was living there. I got so accustomed to the power of the Sword of the Spirit in my mouth, that it was very easy and quick to deal with. The Holy Ghost was always guiding me in what He was doing. I was just following Him.

The wave of His glory is with us, whether we know it or not. He is "the Lord of glory." Everywhere we go, His glory is not only in us, but with us. He is waiting for us to make use of His Word in a deliverance or healing situation. His Word is "quick and powerful". (See Hebrews 4:12) That's why James talks about the power of the tongue. (See James 3:1-18 & Proverbs 18:21) "Death and life are in the power of the tongue." There's power to our words that can enact spiritual realities, whether for good, or for bad. Therefore, we need to learn how to use our tongue appropriately, so that the Lord can fill our mouth with His Word and release His glory in all the earth. He could have chosen to use angels, or chosen to continue to walk the earth and do it Himself, but He has chosen to do it through us. Through us He lives and moves and reaches out to the world and through us He reveals Himself to the world even visibly if that's what it will take to save them.

When people come to us for a prayer for healing or deliverance, they aren't actually coming for us. They are coming for the Power of Christ in us, the hope of the glory. They don't our prayer. They need the Lord of glory to touch them with the gift that He already paid for. No prayers for healing or a miracle can convince God to do something He already wants to do. The glory of God living in us is the very thing that will set the captives free. It's just like when the glory has appears when I am preaching. It imparts great faith to the people who see it. They suddenly put their eyes directly on the Lord of lords, and the King of kings without reserve. "Greater is he that is in us than he that is in the world." (See 1John 4:4) The same glory that was with Him, is with us. (See John 17:22 "And the glory which thou gavest me I have given them." It's Him living inside of us.)

It's the kingdom of God within us and upon us. It's the same Kingdom of God that Jesus sent the seventy to preach about with a demonstration of His Spirit and power in every city and village that He would visit. (See Luke 10:1, 9) That was the power that prepared the way for His coming. It's the same today. He sends us to prepare the way for Him to come. We go and preach the Word to a crowd as small as one and upwards. He confirms it with signs following, revealing to the hearers that He is risen!

1Corinthians 2:4-5

"And my speech and my preaching *was* not with enticing words of man's wisdom, but in demonstration of the Spirit and of power: That your faith should not stand in the wisdom of men, but in the power of God."

When the devils see us, they see the devouring glory of God in the appearance of flames of fire, and they tremble in fear. (See Matthew 8:29; Mark 1:24; Luke 4:34) He came to destroy the works of the devil and He has empowered us to do the same. (See Acts 1:8 & 1John 3:8; John 14:12 & 20:21) "Ye shall receive power after that the Holy Ghost is come upon you: and ye shall be witnesses." The power is for casting out devils, healing the sick and diseased, raising the dead and for signs and wonders to give a witness to Jesus Christ as the only begotten Son of God.

The Oppressor:

1Peter 5:8-11

"Be sober, be vigilant; because your adversary the devil, as a roaring lion, walketh about, seeking whom he may devour: Whom resist steadfast in the faith, knowing that the same afflictions are accomplished in your brethren that are in the world. But the God of all grace, who hath called us unto his eternal glory by Christ Jesus, after that ye have suffered a while, make you perfect, stablish, strengthen, settle *you*. To him *be* glory and dominion for ever and ever. Amen."

The devil(s) goes about as a roaring lion, seeking whom he may oppress. Jesus came to set the captives free from his oppression. (See Luke 4:18, 1John 3:8 & Acts 10:38)

Acts 10:38
"How God anointed Jesus of Nazareth with the Holy Ghost and with power: who went about doing good, and healing all that were oppressed of the devil; for God was with him."

Notice here how that oppression and healing are in the same sentence, thus connecting the two together as one. The oppressor being the source of the oppression which created the need for deliverance and healing. "Healing all that _were_ oppressed of the devil." They _were_ oppressed, until Jesus cast the devil out and healed them. The oppression kept them sick and diseased. Once the oppressor was cast out, the sickness could be healed. Notice also that Jesus was empowered with the Holy Ghost and power to achieve that. The power being: "God was with him," and God is with us. It's the Holy Ghost and power in and upon us to cast out devils and heal all sicknesses and diseases in Jesus name. (See Luke 24:49)

Another verse that shows the same example, is Matthew 8:16-17.

Matthew 8:16-17
"When the even was come, they brought unto him many that were possessed with devils: and he cast out the spirits with *his* word, and healed all that were sick: That it might be fulfilled which was spoken by Esaias the prophet, saying, Himself took our infirmities, and bare *our* sicknesses."

Again, first He cast out the devils and then healed the people that were oppressed with sickness and disease by them.

Devils Oppress Human Flesh:

A Believer in Christ, cannot have a devil in their spirit or soul. They are free in Christ. Nonetheless, their flesh is still subject to oppression from unclean spirits when left unchecked. That doesn't mean that they have a legal right to oppress us, but they go about as a roaring lion seeking whom they may devour. Through the redeeming blood of Jesus that paid the ransom for us, we have salvation for the forgiveness of sins and the penalty of sins, which is the curse of the law (See Galatians 3:13, Deuteronomy 28:15-68 & Revelation 5:9). The curse of the law includes every sickness, disease and calamity that can come our way and swiftly and possibly subtly destroy our lives.

He Gave Himself A Ransom For All:

Matthew 20:28

"Even as the Son of man came not to be ministered unto, but to minister, and to give his life a ransom for many." Many people feel that Jesus came to be ministered to. In fact, the opposite is true. Martha was busy trying to cook Him dinner while Mary sat at His feet hearing His teaching. Jesus wasn't interested in being served the food. He was more interested in serving His people.

1Timothy 2:5-6

"For *there is* one God, and one mediator between God and men, the man Christ Jesus; Who gave himself a ransom for all, to be testified in due time."

John 1:29

"The next day John seeth Jesus coming unto him, and saith, Behold the Lamb of God, which taketh away the sin of the world." He came to take away sin. Not just to cover it up as some believe. He came to actually remove it from us. Praise the Lord! And if we sin again, He acts as a lawyer on our behalf in our defense. (See 1John 2:1-2)

Saved:

The very word "Saved", as used by Jesus Himself, means to be delivered and healed. This was part of the message that He was preaching to the world, as we read in John's Gospel, chapter 3:16-17.

John 3:16-17
"For God so loved the world, that he gave his only begotten Son, that whosoever believeth in him should not perish, but have everlasting life. For God sent not his Son into the world to condemn the world; but that the world through him might be saved **(Gr. To save, deliver or protect, heal, make whole)."**

This is Jesus' message for saving, delivering and healing the sick and the diseased. He preached it and as a result, people came from everywhere to be healed. His message hasn't changed. He's still healing all who come to Him. (See John 6:2 & Matthew 9:35; 14:36; Mark 6:56)

For example:

Matthew 4:23-25
"And Jesus went about all Galilee, teaching in their synagogues, and preaching the gospel of the kingdom, and healing all manner of sickness and all manner of disease among the people. And his fame went throughout all Syria: and they brought unto him all sick people that were taken with divers diseases and torments, and those which were possessed with devils, and those which were lunatic, and those that had the palsy; and he healed them. And there followed him great multitudes of people from Galilee, and *from* Decapolis, and *from* Jerusalem, and *from* Judaea, and *from* beyond Jordan."

The people who were "taken with divers diseases and torments" came to Him. They were oppressed by devils in their flesh and they wanted to be set free. The oppression prevented their flesh from being able to heal itself. They heard of the salvation that Jesus was preaching, saying, "The time is fulfilled, and the kingdom of God is at hand: repent ye, and believe the gospel." (See Mark 1:14-15) and "The Spirit of the Lord is upon me because he hath anointed me to set the captives free." (See

Luke 4:18) The anointing was and is to cast out the oppressing spirits from oppressed flesh. Jesus has all rights in His name to cast them out because He paid the penalty of all sin for all mankind. That means that the devils have no more rights to oppress humanity that turns to Him for salvation. The kingdom God was here then and still is here today. It's the Holy Ghost and power. (See Matthew 12:28 "But if I cast out devils by the Spirit of God, then the kingdom of God is come upon you.") (See also Luke 11:20) (Acts 1:8 "Ye shall receive power, after that the Holy Ghost is come upon you.") We have the legal right in His name to cast stop devils from oppressing those who turn to Jesus for salvation. (See Luke 10:1, 11, 17-19)

Those people in Syria, who weren't even Jews, had heard of Jesus' fame. (See Matthew 4:23-25) They set out all over the country to find ALL that had sickness of any kind. They brought them ALL to Jesus and He healed them ALL. This was Good News for that entire country. Today, it's harder to hear the message of Jesus' fame for what He's doing in setting the captives free from the devils oppression, because Modern-Day-Christians generally believe that Jesus has changed and that He is no longer active on earth. This has to change. We are the ones who are supposed to be sharing the Good News that Jesus is alive, but if we don't have signs following, we lose our credibility. We can save some without them, but those who get saved, without the Power of the Holy Ghost being involved, are likely to become powerless in their witness.

I have been confronted by Modern-Day-Christians too many times regarding the activity of Jesus on earth today. No matter where I go, it always happens and it's the same confrontations every time.

In order for us to represent Him properly, we need to preach the whole Gospel, not just forgiveness of sins. In China, I taught the people that healing is part of salvation and they would be healed at the same time they were forgiven and washed from their sins. It's an all-inclusive package deal and it's free of any cost on our part. Jesus paid the whole price. Many of the Chinese people I ministered to didn't have religious teaching to make them doubt that. Nonetheless, there were those religious teachers who fought against me for preaching healing. They said that Jesus doesn't heal people in their bodies anymore. They believe that He only did that 2,000 years ago. They are blind to the truth and the blind lead the blind and they both fall into a ditch. "Jesus Christ the same yesterday, and today, and forever." (Hebrews 13:8) Nonetheless, even some of those religious preachers changed their minds when they saw the blind eyes open in my meetings. I remember one woman preacher falling to her knees and weeping loudly when she saw a totally blind man from her church cry out, "I can see you brother! I can see your face!!!" In fact, nearly half the church fell to their knees and wept before the Lord when they saw it happen.

Resist the deceptions of the devil in the Modern-Day-Christian churches. We need to stand against it when we are confronted and allow Jesus to set the captives free from the oppression of the devil through us. We need to follow Jesus before following men and women leaders. We need to wake up and let Jesus move through us to save the world.

How Did Jesus Cast Out Devils?

Matthew 12:28
"But if I cast out devils by the Spirit of God, then the kingdom of God is come unto you."

Jesus cast out the devils with the Spirit of God ... think about that ... the Bible can seem to conflict itself if we don't get the revelation of it from the Holy Ghost. In one place we read that Jesus cast out devils with the Word of God. In another place He says that He casts out devils with the "Spirit of God". In Luke He says that He cast out devils with the "finger of God." So is there a difference between the three? No. They are one and the same. The finger of God is attached to the hand of God. Jesus is the hand of God and the Spirit of God at the same time. He is God. He is Lord. He is the Word. You can't separate one from the other. There is one God and not more than one God. He is ONE. As we read in Mark 16:20, that after His resurrection and after His ascension, He was still "working with them, confirming the Word with signs following". How's that possible if He was in Heaven sitting at the right hand of God? It's possible because before He took upon Himself flesh and bone, He was still God and God is a spirit. He is not restricted to His flesh and bone body. He was not the Son of God before

He came to earth. There was no Son of God until He was born with flesh and bone and blood. Before He was the Son of God, He was the Word of God, the coming Christ. He existed as a spirit before He took upon Himself flesh and then He was the only begotten Son of God. It means that He was the only one born with the spirit of God Himself as the person that was dwelling in flesh.

John 1:14 says,

"The Word became flesh and dwelt amongst us."

More Testimonies Of The Power

Chapter 9

There are hundreds of powerful testimonies that I could share from my time in China, but I can only share a small number in this volume. Therefore, I decided to add a chapter of a summary of some of the highlights during my time there.

There was a young Chinese woman who was friends with one of my translators. She had spent two years doing ministry help and training in a well-known movement in the US that was involved in some 24 hour prayer seven days a week for such a long time. While she was there, apparently there was a revival happening, yet when I asked her if she even had seen or experienced the actual fire of God, she said she hadn't. Nonetheless, when she was in one of my ministry team training sessions, I asked her to pray for those needing healing and a blessing. I had the class line up and she went along the back of each one to lay hands on them. She was a very nice Chinese girl from Shanghai and very sincere in her desire to know more about Jesus and to be used by Him, so I was surprised that after two years in her ministry training, she still was not sure that the Lord would heal others through her when she laid her hands on them in Jesus name.

As soon as she began to lay hands on the team members, she looked at me and said, "I feel fire on my hands!" She was so sweet, trying to remain calm and appear so confident in the training she had, but this was completely different from anything she learned during her two years training. The team members were being touched and healed from things that they themselves may have been waiting for the Lord to heal by faith. Many of them had already experienced healing in their bodies and salvation in their families, but there were still some little things that needed to be completed in them. I remember one girl that she laid hands on had back issues still, but when the girl laid hands on her back, the fire of God healed her instantly. She was so surprised but kept her posture and didn't act surprised.

Later that day, where we were driving this dear sister to the train station to go home to Shanghai, she suddenly blurted out, saying, "Wasn't that amazing!" I said, "Yes, but let me ask you this: in all the time in your training, did you ever experience the power of the glory of God that way." She replied, with a humble smile, saying, "No, never ... not once in the two years that I was there did I ever experience the power of God that way through myself nor did I see it happen that way through others in that time."

Praise the Lord! The Lord is the fire and the fire is a shining light. He came to restore all that was lost through Adams fall, and it's obvious that a little religious talk isn't enough to do that. We need the Power of God to do that. (See 1Corinthians 2:4-5) That light shines in the darkness and all those that are still in the darkness comprehend it not! (See John 1:5) What's the Light? It's the Word of God ... it's not an intellectual thing ... it's God Himself ... I've seen the fire of God with open eyes before ... it's a bright a shining light ... I've seen it going throughout a meeting and seeking whom would receive it ... I've seen it approach people and turn away and go to the next because they weren't open to it. I've seen it enter into others and remain there. Sometimes people claim to see a bright white light and think that it's some kind of angel, but they are mistaken ... it's the Word of God as a bright shining light ... God is a spirit ... it's no wonder that I receive revelation from Him all day long ... because I'm open to Him in ways that others cannot imagine ... I'm not bound by religious thinking and religious ways ... I know Him and He knows me in a personal way ... We are not strangers to each other ...

It used to be that occasionally, I would fear to lose my salvation because I thought I may be one of those whom Jesus rejects when they said to Him, "Lord, Lord, did we not cast out devils in your name" And Jesus reply to them was, "I never knew you." But thank the Lord that I know Him personally, not just intellectually! Because I still hear His voice tell me, "I'm your Lord and your friend". It's at that time that I feel assured again of my salvation in Christ … His voice to me brings me the peace that passes all understanding … Thank You Jesus! He wants the same for all His children. We have so much in Christ, but the devil wants to steal it from us and use it for His own benefit, just as He stole the spiritual blessings from Adam and Eve.

A couple months after the sweet Chinese girl had experienced the fire, she came back to the city where I was. This time she brought her mother who needed healing. My translator and I joined them and some other preachers for dinner that night. The young girl told me that her mother was totally deaf in one ear and had only partial hearing in the other ear. She asked me to lay hands on her, so I did, in Jesus name, and her ears were instantly opened! The girl didn't believe her mother's testimony and asked her mother to repeat the words she spoke to her. She did! No problem! So then the daughter asked me to lay hands for her mother's eyes because she had very poor vision. Her mother was wearing glasses and I asked her to take them off and I laid hands on her eyes and commanded the blind spirit to go in Jesus name. Then she tested her eyes without the glasses and she said that she could see clearly! Wow! Can you say Wow!? It means, "Hallelujah!"

I'm not in contact with this young girl ever since that day, and so I have no idea of how these events impacted her or her mother's life, but I'm sure that those two encounters changed their lives more than the two years with that group that were in their rut of worship 24/7. Worship is awesome! I practice it every day … but I don't park there … praise and worship are launching pads for us to go forth and do all that Jesus did and greater things than that! … I go onto greater things in Christ … Praise and worship helps us to get tuned into His fellowship … we need that very very much … but after we've done that, we need to let our light so shine before men so that they can see our works and glorify God (See Matthew 516) … If that isn't happening in our lives, then we are stuck in a rut … let's get out of that rut! And glorify God with the Good Works of Christ in us, the hope of glory. (See Colossians 1:27) Jesus said, "The works that I do shall you do also." (See John 14:12) Those are the works that He's talking about. The works He did were signs and wonders that caused people to marvel. (See Matthew 9:8)

We spend time in daily praise and worship and prayer to learn to hear His leading. This is essential for us to live the Life that He offers us as Believers in Christ, but don't forget that the devils come to steal the seed that we sow into our spirit, with the cares of this world. (See Mark 4:19) We can protect that word of God that we plant in our spirits by receiving the understanding of it by the Holy Ghost. Matthew 13:19 "When any one heareth the word (logos) of the kingdom, and understandeth *it* not, then cometh the wicked *one*, and catcheth away that which was sown in his heart. This is he which received seed by the way side (hard ground)." We need to read the Word of God daily to remind ourselves that we are not of this world and that Jesus overcame this world. We need to walk in the victory of Christ. That's our inheritance. We need to continually seek Him and His guidance in our lives. (See John 16:13)

I wish I had more time to keep adding to this compilation of my time in China, but my time has run out. In the meantime, I will keep writing and in preparation for the next book, which I believe will be called: "Canada Invaded By Heaven." I believe that this is the next work He has called me to and that I have been preparing for the past three years since I returned from China. I expect that what the Lord begins, He will also complete.

Revival of the Baptism of the Holy Ghost and Fire

It was two months before I was leaving China to come home. I had seen hundreds of miracles, clouds of glory becoming visible to the entire church, the wind blowing in every meeting, and feeling the fire of the Holy Ghost fall in the meetings. Then one day, I saw something I had never seen before. There was a bright cloud in one of the isles in the church where I had my weekly Tuesday Miracle Meetings. It was so bright that I could hardly look at it without hurting my eyes. At first I thought it was just a reflection from the sun, but after a few minutes,

I realized that it couldn't be the sun's reflection, because there was nothing for the sun to reflect off of that would make such a bright light. That's when I decided to look closer at it. I kept preaching, but looked closely at the bright light with my eyes only open a little. Then to my amazement, I saw a brilliant flame burning in the midst of a cloud on the floor! The Lord spoke to me at that moment, saying, "I want to do a revival of the baptism of the Holy Ghost and Fire. Begin preaching this at every meeting and invite all to come and receive it."

Since that day, I began doing just as He said, and every person in every church where I preached for the first time, came forward to receive it. I preached it simple, because these people generally never heard that there is a baptism of the Holy Ghost today, let alone the baptism of the Holy Ghost fire. I would preach to them from the book of Ephesians 3:20-21, saying

Ephesians 3:20-21 "Now unto him that is able to do exceeding abundantly above all that we ask or think, according to the power that worketh in us, Unto him *be* glory in the church by Christ Jesus throughout all ages, world without end. Amen."

I read this and other verses to them, such as Acts 1:8, saying, "Ye shall receive power after that the Holy Ghost has come upon YOU!" I would then ask them if they wanted to experience having their prayers answered exceedingly above all that they ask or think, and they all said yes. I told them, "Then you need the baptism of the Holy Ghost and Fire that's the promise of the Father to you and is confirmed by the apostle Paul in Ephesians 3:20, saying, "According to the power that worketh in us." If you want that power to work in you, they raise your hand." Everyone always raised their hand, and I then asked them all to come forward, or we went outside often if there was no room for them to come forward.

Before I laid hands on each one of them, I would ask them, "How many of you are feeling the Holy Ghost fire burning upon your heads?" and every hand always went up. I would say, "How many of you are feeling the wind of the Holy Ghost blowing upon you now?" and most hands wet up. Some would testify to it. I always opened the floor for people to give testimony to what they were experiencing and when they shared, it would build people's faith to know that Jesus was Himself in our midst through His Holy Spirit.

The Lord is so wanting to spread the Good News of the Kingdom of Heaven at hand in the world today. It's everything that He promised in our midst NOW. It's the activity of His Holy Spirit in our midst. It's the Pentecostal outpouring, but it's only experienced by faith, so if we don't have faith for it, we feel like we are left out. God isn't leaving anyone out. People perish for a lack of knowledge the Bible says. I'm like a child in His presence. I believe that He will do all that He said He would do and I believe that I can do all that He said I can do. The difficulty for me is not in the believing department. The difficulty is the religious leaders who know nothing or very little of Pentecost experientially that try to resist the Holy Ghost. They want to be the first or last to experience it and yet they have never experienced it, and when one who does experience comes in their midst, they become jealous of it in us and oppose the Spirit of God in us. They have no idea that they are in fact opposing Jesus Himself.

There's a solution, and this is the solution that I personally feel led by the Lord to do: The solution for me personally, is the same here in Canada as it was in China. In China, I had so much opposition from the religious leadership. They opposed the Holy Ghost preaching. One of them reported me to the government and they came looking for me. Fortunately for me, I had already left the country. I was confronted by preachers while I was preaching. I had to set them record straight by using the Word of God against their rebukes while I was preaching. Some of them resigned or lost their position for opposing the Lord in me. Today in Canada, I still experience the same opposition from leadership, but that won't stop me from preaching the True Gospel of Christ with signs following. Pentecost is a living present fact and it must be preached all the time. The Kingdom of God and the resurrection of Christ must be preached all the time. The baptism of the Holy Ghost and Fire must be preached all the time. The people don't just need some teaching from the Word of God. They need to learn how to walk in the Word of God experientially. Therefore, the preachers also need to know how to walk in the Word of God experientially. That means, Pentecost, which is what Jesus came to fulfill for His people to live in communion with Him in every realm of life. Without Pentecost being active each and every one of our lives, we are just acting like we are Christians. Christians are the ones who are walking in the Power of Christ. That's what a Christian is. Christians were called Christians because they turned the world upside down.

In the last two churches that I preached, there was over 1,000 people in attendance. I had invited all the people in each church to receive the baptism of the Holy Ghost and fire near the beginning of the message, and every hand went up in the air. After I finished preaching the Gospel of the Baptism of the Holy Ghost and Fire to them, I asked them, how many felt tongues of fire upon their heads. Every hand went up! So in reality, there were probably much more than 1,000 souls that received it in my time there.

One very important thing I discovered in preaching the Gospel of the Kingdom of God, is that if you don't even fully believe it, but you know it's the truth, just preach it anyways, and the Lord WILL confirm it with signs following. There were many times that I felt doubt to the message, but I preached it anyways, because I knew that it's true, whether I felt faith for it at that moment or not. He confirms the Word, not our feelings. I learned to not let my feelings get in the way of preaching His message boldly. We all have issues that come up in life, but though we may change, His Word never changes. We simply need to stick to His Word and we will be sure to have victory.

I live in Brampton Ontario, and will be beginning an evangelistic campaign as a hobby for the sake of the Gospel of Christ, as soon as this book has been published. If you feel that the Lord is calling you to start an evangelistic campaign as a hobby as a result of reading this book, feel free to contact me to team up with me in Christ to make it happen. I will help you in whatever way I can, including sharing with you more of what the Lord has shown me in how to do it successfully.

To Contact Me:

Through:

Facebook: johnwaterhouse.333@gmail.com

Twitter: 333Waterhouse

Email: johnwaterhouse.333@gmail.com

Website: www.johnwaterhouse333.com

Please feel free to send any questions or testimonies you have and I will be sure to respond as quickly as possible.

God Bless you and make His face to shine upon you, in Jesus name. Amen!

Your Brother in Christ,

John Waterhouse

Every scripture reference in this book is from the KJV. None are taken from the NKJV or any other Bible.

Edwards Brothers Malloy
Oxnard, CA USA
October 20, 2014